# 10 Tips on How **NOT** to Talk to Your Kids about Sex

Blessings,
Audrey Werner

Audrey Werner has written a refreshing, readable book on sexuality for churches and for parents to help them grapple with the unrelenting attack on purity they and their children face daily. It is a blessing to know it can be read without fear or shame, but Godly enlightening.

DR. JUDITH REISMAN

Author, *Kinsey, Sex and Fraud, "Soft" Porn Plays Hard Ball*; Founder of the Institute for Media Education; Director, Child Protection Institute, Liberty University School of Law

I wish I had been able to study the information in this powerful, positive, palatable book years ago when I was raising my children. It would have reduced my husband's and my stress talking about the sensitive subject of sex. But, it's not too late for our grandchildren. Take the embarrassment and stress out of this necessary task! Read this book and see how positive it is to talk about this subject God's way.

DR. THELMA WELLS

Founder, A Woman of God Ministries and Generation Love-Divine Explosion; Speaker, Author, Professor, TV Host (NRB and TBN Television); former "Women of Faith" Conference Speaker

In this book, Audrey Werner uses the words 'purity' and 'pure' more than sixty times. Her theme reflects the core Biblical standard for living the highest, wisest, most satisfying and ennobling life possible. That is the kind of life loving parents want for their children. It is the kind of life the Heavenly Father wants for His children.

Purity of body, mind, and spirit are the core components of an ennobling existence. For most young people, the body gets far more attention than the mind or the spirit—it's a fact of human existence. It stands to reason that maintaining purity of the body during one's youth is mostly focused on sexuality. The outcome of that focus has the greatest impact on the development of the mind and spirit.

What you will learn about sexual purity by reading this book may very well change your entire understanding of what the Psalmist meant when he addressed youth's most critical challenge: 'How can a young man [person] keep his way pure? By keeping it according to Your word' (Psalm 119:9).

DR. DENNIS FREY

President, Master's International University of Divinity

Eunice and I appreciate your love of God and Country. Your dedication is exemplary. Your love of our children born and unborn is remarkable, and your work of educating the Church on behalf of restoring legal protections for marriage, women and children is gratifying. Thanks for all you do for the RSVP America, First Principles Press, and Matthew XVIII.

COL. RONALD D. RAY
USMCR (Ret.), Deputy Assistant Secretary of Defense during the Reagan Administration

Thank you Audrey Werner for carrying the torch forward to awaken the church which, so often, is a thankless mission. Colonel Ray always said there's a banality to evil. It is only reintroduced in a thin disguise in each generation, but it's the same old hell that's been lurking since the Garden. The RSVP America archive became the focus of our work in 2006, after actively pursuing the campaign from 1998-2003. We were directed to sort, scan and upload thousands of documents—all of the RSVP America papers and materials—to serve as 'crumbs along the path' for future generations to follow so they don't have to rediscover the fraud and crime that changed Godly American law and public policy that once protected Marriage, Women, and Children. Audrey, your Matthew XVIII work continues to call attention to the good news of God's perfect plan for the Marriage institution and its protections for His most vulnerable.

EUNICE RAY
Founder and Director, RSVP America

I have seen the results of a generation taught sex education from a personal, spiritual, and societal view point. *10 Tips on How NOT to Talk to Your Kids about Sex* makes objective what I have known through personal and pastoral experience. Audrey gives us a good guide for parents to both protect their children from the assaults of the devil and the world, and to teach them purity according to the Word of God. I recommend this book not only for parents, but also for church professionals and leaders, so that all of us might wake up to the dangers of sex education, even when it is cloaked in 'Christian' verbiage.

MARK CUTLER
Pastor, Trinity Lutheran Church, Kalispell, Montana

Activists are continually polluting the minds of children under the guise of "Sex Education." This abuse has to stop. The Matthew XVIII Group is a critical ministry to help parents discover the truth behind the agenda and empower them to protect the innocence of their children. Audrey Werner reminds me of a modern-day Esther. She is called for "such a time as this" to boldly present her case before king and country for the saving of many lives. She has worked with legislators all over the world to help restore Biblical purity to our hurting world.

KENDRA WHITE
Producer, American Family Studios

It has been said that God uses people in all stages of His work: those who plant the seed, those who water, while God causes all things to grow. So it is with Audrey's book. Audrey watered faithfully year after year!

More than twenty years ago I asked Audrey to look at the *Learning About Sex* series from CPH. As a Mom, I was greatly disturbed and angered by the content of these books. Audrey was equally incensed, but the scale of influence Audrey brought to this endeavor was monumental. I love how God prepared Audrey for this mission. He wove her talents and interests in the medical field and she became a nurse. But not just any kind of nurse—a County Health nurse. He gave her all sorts of experiences that solidified her ability to speak with authority on the subject. He also enflamed her with a love of His Word—and it was weaving the two together that makes this book so monumentally important.

Christians have been deceived by the world's 'knowledge'. Audrey has replaced it with God knowledge! So much more effective and so much more rewarding for parents. May your life and the lives of your children be blessed by this book. My prayer is that after reading this book you recognize the lies of the world and take a stand for your children. Well done, Audrey, this has become your lifelong mission—saving the innocence of young souls!

PATRICIA RAEZLER
Director, Westmaple Preschool

We parents, today, are raising our children immersed in a culture of every kind of sexual depravity. On top of that, most of us haven't even experienced true purity, ourselves. A spirit of confusion moves powerfully, even amongst the faithful. *10 Tips on How NOT to Talk to Your Kids about Sex* shines the light of God's Word on all of these matters, and brings them into crystal clear focus.

ROEL & ROBYN VAN ECK
Parents of 9 children

I have had the privilege, on multiple occasions, of experiencing firsthand, Prof. Audrey Werner's ministry to a wide spectrum of people ranging from university students and religious leaders, to Honorable Members of Parliament.

One thing that stands out, is the way her ministry literally opens people's eyes to the destructive impact of the sex revolution around them, which they had attributed to other causes. Prof. Werner, earlier in her career, was trained, unbeknownst to her, to teach children the harmful comprehensive sexuality education, and personally witnessed its negative consequences on a wide range of children including Christian children. Based on that knowledge and experience, she conducted extensive research on the origins and impact of the sex revolution. Following from that, she now makes a compelling submission to go back to Biblical standards of morality and purity, in a manner that few can match today.

While most leaders in today's world are obsessed with political correctness at the expense of their national destruction, Prof. Werner is not shy to remind the world what the founders of the Western civilization understood; and history, too, confirms through studies conducted by world renown social scientists, that, morality is a national security issue.

Prof. Werner exposes the deceptive and manipulative strategies used by the promoters of the sex revolution movement. She reveals how they use radical sex education programs to advance their hidden agenda of deliberately destroying families, the moral fibre of society and in the process, de-Christianizing the world and building a new world order based on sexual anarchy.

Through her ministry and book, "10 Tips on How Not to Talk to Your Kids about Sex", Prof. Werner offers the solution to this failed social engineering experiment, as going back to battletested and proven Biblical purity and moral standards. From this foundation, Prof. Werner convincingly presents the case for equipping and empowering parents to teach their children matters relating to purity. She further argues that schools should only be limited to teaching about human reproduction in biology classes purely from an academic point of view, just as it was before the introduction of sex education in schools in 1964. She points out the disturbing reality that it was the porn industry developers and people associated with the fraudulent studies and warped ideology of human sexuality carried out by Alfred Kinsey in the 1940's, that lay the foundation and developed the sex education curriculum. Prof. Werner explains that this is where the sex education taught in schools and youth groups originates. And that this is what informs the various categories of sex education, sexuality education, comprehensive sexuality education and now the sexual and reproductive health and rights programs around the world.

From her book, Prof. Werner stresses the importance of applying the principle of modesty and using modest language just as the Bible does. She implores her audience to understand how the Bible cherishes the protection of the innocence of children, which confirms the fact that every child has an "internal clock" that governs their growth in the God-given gift of our sexuality.

I therefore highly recommend Prof. Werner's ministry and book to parents, religious leaders of all faiths, legislators, politicians, educators, youth workers and anyone interested in understanding how we got to where we are now as a global community, and how to counter the damage that the sex revolution and radical sex education has done in our communities and nations.

STEPHEN & BEATRICE LANGA

President (and President's wife) of Family Life Network, Uganda

# 10 Tips on
# How **NOT** to Talk to Your Kids about Sex

Audrey Werner

**The Matthew XVIII Group**

A Purity Paradigm For
Our Homes, Churches, and Nations

10 Tips on How NOT to Talk to Your Kids about Sex, Revised Edition.


Printed in the United States of America
**ISBN:** 979-8-9850692-0-4

**Cover Design:** Lisa Thomson, Roel van Eck
**Cover Artwork:** Shutterstock
**Interior Design:** Lisa Thomson, Robyn van Eck



**Published by:**
The Matthew XVIII Group
www.matthewxviii.org

For more information on this title, or for permission requests,
visit www.matthewxviii.org.

*Dedicated*
*to my children,*
*their generation,*
*and future generations*

# Contents

# Foreword

by Anne Marie Ezzo

As parents and educators, it's important to understand that "sexual knowledge" is not innocent knowledge, because sexual knowledge cannot be separated from moral knowledge that regulates human emotions and responses.

Every child has the right to live in a safe world where he or she is not assaulted physically, emotionally, sexually or morally—a world where a child is not taken advantage of or over-powered and forced to accept unsolicited teaching regarding his or her sexuality.

But how do we protect children from intrusive, uninvited, inappropriate forces that can injure their emotional and moral capacities? Who determines what is inappropriate, what is good, reasonable, protective—and what crosses the line? What can and should parents be doing at home to protect and prepare their children for the moral and sexual onslaught prevalent in our current society, without robbing their children of their innocence? Or, as the current generation of parents are being told, "Leave it to the professionals and we'll provide your children comprehensive sex education classes in the comfort of their classroom."

Because of the subject matter, many parents are all too willing to abdicate their position of primary teacher and influencer of their children. They believe the lie that the "experts" have a better way, and therefore release their children to hear information that introduces them to vocabulary and concepts about their sexual identity that a previous generation couldn't have dreamed of. Nor would they have even known the meanings of half of what is being taught to today's children as "fact."

While parents in the twenty-first century are attempting to process all these changes regarding our sexuality, most are completely unaware of where this whole sex ed thing began. After all, it would have been during their parents' youth, starting back in 1964, that the idea of sex education was introduced into the public sector: information based on research by a Dr. Alfred Kinsey. It was his "scientific studies" that provided a new view of sexuality outside the context of marriage and children. Prior to Kinsey, writings that reflected the American notion of human sexuality were presented as **God's Life Process** or the **Marital Act**, and everything else was known as **Carnal Knowledge**. We went from viewing man as an individual created in the image of God—with dignity and what we call biblical anthropological context—to viewing man as part of Zoology, just higher up in the animal kingdom.

So, we ask, "How can we teach our children a biblical view of sexuality, when from a very early age they are saturated with details and images that constantly challenge the very concept of biblical purity?" Before that question can be answered, parents and educators need to understand how we got here—and then what we can do about it. That is what Audrey Werner is presenting in *10 Tips on How NOT to Talk to Your Kids about Sex*.

Within the pages of this book Audrey shares not only her own journey of discovery about the foundations of the current sex education movement, but also the agenda behind it. As you read Audrey's systematic and logical progression, the evidence becomes overwhelming that America is on the wrong track when it comes to sex education. Your emotions may go between anger at being duped by the experts, to helplessness in thinking, *But how can I make a difference and what can be done now?!* Well, if enough of us join Audrey, and others, in this battle, we can make a difference. Audrey herself has said, "Who am *I*? I'm just a mom." Well, there is nothing like waking up the "Mama bear" in every Mom who finds out her precious children's innocence is being violated—all under the guise of "education."

Audrey Werner, RN, B.S.N., M.A. and MOM, decided to make a difference as one ordinary person seeking Truth. Within *10 Tips on How NOT to Talk to Your Kids about Sex*, she will expose the darkness presented through Kinsey's fraudulent science that has found its way into Christian sex education materials, and then inspire you as a parent and educator to return to sharing with children about God's life process in a modest, biblical way. As a parent educator for over thirty years, I am confident this will be one of those books that will be life changing for you, your children, and yes—even your grandchildren.

**For such a time as this** are we living—and we can make a difference.

**Anne Marie Ezzo**
Author and Co-Founder of
Growing Families International

# Preface

Did the title catch you off guard? *How **NOT** to Talk to Your Kids about Sex?* The typical theme today is *How **to** Talk to Your Kids about Sex*. Some well-meaning Christians add to that title, *...from a Biblical Perspective*, or they use the term, "biblical sexuality." But how much of the information they share is *biblical*, and how much is from man's hollow, deceptive philosophy?

How do you feel about giving your child the "sex talk?" Are you uncomfortable at the thought of it—or even dreading it? Do you have memories of your parent squirming through this talk with you, or did they throw a book at you and tell you to read it? Then, once you received "the talk," do you remember how you felt? Were you grossed out, disgusted, or were other emotions awakened in you?

Parents, today you are being encouraged to get over or push through any discomfort and give "the talk" because you need to make sure that your kids know about sex before someone else tells them. But do you wonder why you have this discomfort?

What if I told you that leaders from Planned Parenthood (the world's largest abortion industry), the American Humanist Association, and those who support pedophilia and pornography were behind the development of sex education? Would that make you feel better about talking to your kids graphically about sex? I would hope not!

As parents, we want what is best for our children. Honest research and history have shown that the traditional family has always been the foundation of any successful nation. People who limit themselves to one partner and delay sex until marriage have no venereal diseases at all and seem not only to stay married longer but to have a stronger commitment to the institution of marriage. Research and history have also proven that children thrive in homes where there is a mom and dad under one roof.

These are crazy times. Responsibilities have been replaced with *sexual rights*, and God's Word has been replaced with *feelings*. We live in a world with the theme, "If it feels good, do it;" and sexual agendas are being promoted daily in schools and through the media.

How do we protect our children from a world thrown into moral chaos, and how do we prepare our children for the best possible outcome? Should we educate them in sex? In abstinence? Or should we educate them in purity? Facing all of these difficult decisions can feel like an overwhelming burden.

There is hope! We have the most powerful tool available to us, and that is God's Word. That tool is more powerful than any double-edged sword.[1] In Ephesians 6:17, Paul refers to it as "the sword of the Spirit, which is the Word of God." Many Christians today underestimate the power of this tool, but it is the place where we will find the answers to these questions.

The problem with many Christian resources today is that oftentimes unaware, authors have attempted to mesh God's Word with words from worldly, atheistic "experts on sex". Years of research have revealed to me that these "experts" had a plan to sexualize a nation they believed to be too Victorian and repressed. After decades of their influence, our society has come to be characterized by rampant sexual immorality, even within the church.

God advises His people:

> If My people who are called by My name, will humble themselves, and pray and seek My face, and *turn from their wicked ways*, then I will hear from heaven, and will forgive their sin and heal their land. (2 Chronicles 7:14)

---

[1] Hebrews 4:12.

In this book I hope to prove why we can no longer rely on the deadly combination which has been named "Human Sexuality from a biblical perspective." It has been especially disastrous in the area of sex education, where vulnerable children have been exposed to materials that not only were intended to awaken love before its time,[2] but have taught the last few generations to replace biblical love with lust.

We are at a critical point in our nation, where Christians are now being asked to "go into the closet." We are being told no longer to adhere to God's biblical standards but to accept new and evolving morality. Religious freedom is in jeopardy, and we need the Lord now more than ever to intervene; but we have a vital part to play in this work as well.

It is my prayer that this book gives you answers and true scriptural reference, void of man's philosophy, on what we are to convey to our children. It is my prayer that parents will be able to equip their children, using God's Word, to take on the devil's schemes and help their children remain pure for the man or woman God intended them to be with. It is my prayer that young people will be immersed in seeking out God's plan for their lives and not be involved in various sexual sins.

If parents become the primary educators of their children again and teach God's standard of purity, this generation of children can restore what the cankerworm has eaten away. God's design for the family can be restored, and God's people can influence the world around them for good and not evil.

> Only be strong and very courageous, that you may observe to do according to all the law which Moses My servant commanded you; do not turn from it to the right hand or to the left, that you may prosper wherever you go. (Joshua 1:7)

---

[2] Song of Songs 2:7; 3:5, 8:4.

# Introduction

October, 2001. God was opening up a new mission for me. I silently marveled as I found myself in a security check line at O'Hare International Airport for a day trip—destination Des Moines, Iowa.

I was to meet up with a ministry partner. I had been pursuing a certain publishing company for the past few years, and this ministry partner had been instrumental in setting up a long-awaited audience with them. I was finally being given an invitation into the inner sanctum. This would grant me the opportunity to present important information—information with a broad, multi-generational impact.

Flying post-September 11, 2001, security was high, the lines long, and the wait even longer. I read Ezekiel 33 while waiting in line, as an assignment from a man who had become a friend and mentor during those years—the former Deputy Assistant to the Secretary of Defense under President Reagan, Col. Ron Ray.

> Again the word of the Lord came to me, saying, "Son of man, speak to the children of your people, and say to them: 'When I bring the sword upon a land, and the people of the land take a man from their territory and make him their watchman, when he sees the sword coming upon the land, if he blows the trumpet and warns the people, then whoever hears the sound of the trumpet and does not take warning, if the sword comes and takes him away, his blood shall be on his own head. ... But if the watch-

> man sees the sword coming and does not blow the trumpet, and the people are not warned, and the sword comes and takes any person from among them, he is taken away in his iniquity; but his blood I will require at the watchman's hand.'
>
> "So you, son of man: I have made you a watchman for the house of Israel; therefore you shall hear a word from My mouth and warn them for Me. When I say to the wicked, 'O wicked man, you shall surely die!' and you do not speak to warn the wicked from his way, that wicked man shall die in his iniquity; but his blood I will require at your hand. Nevertheless if you warn the wicked to turn from his way, and he does not turn from his way, he shall die in his iniquity; but you have delivered your soul."[1]

I knew the stakes were high. This little chapter prepared me for the mission before me, and it was to become my marching orders going forward—to be "one who warns... a watchman on the wall."

What was my mission? What was the information I had come to share? I had come to unveil the lies at the foundation of the sex education series, *Learning About Sex*. This material, published by the conservative Lutheran denomination's own publishing company, was not based on fact but fiction. Yet it had been instrumental in setting the trajectory for Christian sex education over the previous thirty years, creating a situation where their publications and policy, based on deceit, had negatively influenced three decades of children—in all of the Christian denominations. The leaders of this publishing company needed to hear the truth to prevent another three decades of harm![2]

*How on earth did I get here?*

I am thankful to have been raised in a solid Christian home, and educated in Christian schools. I knew my calling was to be a nurse, so after I graduated I went to nursing school, and then became an ER nurse. In God's perfect timing, I married a wonderful, loving man who was a Youth and later Family Life Minister in the Lutheran Church; and then I became a school nurse.

---

[1] Ezekiel 33:1-9.

[2] See the *LAS* review at https://www.matthewxviii.org/curriculum-review.

The funny thing about being a school nurse was that part of my job was to teach the sex ed classes. This wasn't what I had signed up for, but during my training I learned how important sex ed was for children. I had grown up in the 60s and 70s, and changes were happening in our society—unwed pregnancy and STDs had been a shocking scandal, almost unheard of, in my youth; but now these things were sharply on the rise. I learned that sex education would solve the rising unwed birth and STD crisis, by helping youth understand these things better and make better choices.

After a few years, my life took another turn—predictable, but life-changing. I became a mother. I wanted to cut back on nursing to part-time so I could spend more time at home with my precious baby, and that is where God had a very big surprise in store for me... The only part-time nursing position available in my area was in an STD clinic. I was thankful for the opportunity to keep nursing while spending more time with my baby, so I gladly took the job.

I worked at this STD clinic for eight years, from 1991 to 1999. What I saw there shocked me.

When I began working at the STD clinic in 1991, the patients coming in who were involved in unmarried sex were usually troubled by shame and guilt; but by the time I left only eight years later, all of the guilt and shame were gone. The attitudes of our patients completely changed... In only eight years! One of the services we provided was performing court-ordered HIV tests on men accused of rape. Not pleasant, but part of the job. But by the time I left, we weren't just running HIV tests on men accused of rape, we were running court-ordered tests on *boys* accused of rape. When I began my work as an STD nurse, the average age of first sexual contact for our patients was 16; eight years later, it was not uncommon for a patient's first sexual contact to occur at age 10.

Meanwhile, working with the youth at church, my husband was seeing many of the same things: abortions, teen pregnancy, pornography, sexually transmitted disease, and even prostitution. We scratched our heads in confusion, asking, *Whatever happened to chastity and purity?* What hope was there for our children and their peers?

I didn't realize it fully at the time, but God had orchestrated this career path: He was showing me the fruit of the work I had done "educating" children in sexuality. I had sown the seed of sex ed in children's minds, and now God was letting me see the fruit that seed had borne—not *less* unwed pregnancy and STDs, but *more*.

When my son began elementary school in our local private Christian school, the children were going to be taught the same Christian sex ed curriculum I had been taught when I went to that school; so I requested to teach purity to the other parents at my school, to make them aware of the things I was learning. I was beginning to smell a rat, and I didn't want my son getting bitten!

Little did I know that that request—to teach purity at our local Christian school—was going to turn my life upside down.

I would present to the parents of our school before the children went through the program, and I... Well, what can I say? I'm a researcher. I wanted to be prepared to tell my fellow parents about what I was seeing; so I started digging into statistics and history to get a clearer picture about what was going on. But the more I dug, the more digging I discovered there was to be done. It was like pulling back the layers of an onion, continually finding more beneath every layer I uncovered.

It turned out that sex ed was *harming* kids.

It turned out that sex ed was created by *pedophiles* and other sexual deviants; it was intentionally designed to harm kids.

It turned out that even "Christian" sex ed was based on the fraudulent information put out by these perverted people.

And there was more. So much more.

At one point in those early days, the head of the local Planned Parenthood clinic wrote in our newspaper, encouraging parents to sexualize their kids by teaching them graphic sex ed. In response, I wrote a letter to the editor, explaining about some of the things I had learned. The next week, our smalltown newspaper printed a response penned... by the head of the Kinsey Institute![3] How did the head of the Kinsey Institute even hear about this little letter to the editor? And even if he had somehow seen my offering, how did a little letter to the editor in a smalltown newspaper

---

[3] Alfred Kinsey is considered the Father of the Sexual Revolution; more about him in Part I.

rate as important enough that the head of the Kinsey Institute had felt the need to take the time to write out a response to it?

Clearly, I had hit a nerve.

For four years, I researched; I taught; I wrote. I was just a mom, but who else was going to expose this? God had led me on this path, and I could not keep quiet about what I was learning. In the meantime, He provided amazing connections for me—the leading Kinsey expert in the world, the founder of RSVP America, and, yes, the former Deputy Assistant to the Secretary of Defense under Ronald Reagan!

On that morning back in October 2001, a wife, mom, and former public health nurse headed to the Lutherans for Life headquarters to make a presentation and a plea. Armed with documents that would do well as a Supreme Court brief, an appeal was made to Concordia Publishing House: "Please pull your sex education curriculum. You are in error, and are publishing lies that are harming children; please wake up and hear the truth." Concerned for integrity in the Church, I left them with four action points, including removal of the sex education series and development of a program that promotes chastity and purity. Without change, what future would there be for my children?

That week in October, my warning fell on deaf ears. Yet despite the unwillingness of Lutheran leaders to hear about the lies and deception in their sex education curriculum, God continued to put me in situations where I could warn the church—from Christian moms and dads to pastors and denominational leaders—about the dangers of the sex education that is being taught to Christian kids.

In Matthew 18:15–17, Jesus says,

> "Moreover if your brother sins against you, go and tell him his fault between you and him alone. If he hears you, you have gained your brother. But if he will not hear, take with you one or two more, that 'by the mouth of two or three witnesses every word may be established.' And if he refuses to hear them, tell it to the church."

My prayer is that as you read this book, God will direct your thoughts like He did mine—that you will undergo a *purity paradigm shift*. Today, the Lord has brought many of us out of the worldview of sex ed and the Sexual Revolution; may He do the same now for you and your children.

# Part I:

# Know Your History!

Chapter 1

# The Background

> My people are destroyed for lack of knowledge: because you have rejected knowledge, I also will reject you from being priest for Me: because you have forgotten the law of your God, I also will forget your children. (Hosea 4:6)

Before we go any further, we have to address the elephant in the room: In order to understand the 10 Tips, you've got to understand where we came from and how we got here. So in a very real sense, the first Tip, which you need before all of the other Tips, is this: Know Your History!

As a certified sex educator, my job became teaching sex education everywhere—from public schools to Sunday School, from elementary school to high school. Part of my sex ed certification process had included learning why it was important to do this teaching. Our class was told, "Parents aren't doing their job. We now have 'sexuality experts' in the field who have more knowledge than the parents, and we will be following their dictates." So parents and others who worked with children all looked to the "expert" (me) to do this right, and I dutifully taught the children just as I'd been trained to.

The "sexuality experts" who conducted our training told us that by educating children in their sexuality, we would help decrease teen STD (sexually transmitted disease) and pregnancy rates. However, no matter how faithfully we followed what the experts proposed, we never saw the promised fruit.

For five years I worked as a sex educator. Then, in God's providence, I started working as a nurse in an STD clinic.

Our daily work at the STD clinic was to administer STD, HIV, and pregnancy tests, as well as to counsel rape victims and related work of this sort. Day by day, year by year, the true results of the sex ed training I had received by the "experts" became more evident: Not only were the experts' promises proving to be hollow, the opposite was coming true. The more and earlier that sex education was given to children, the more and earlier children became sexually active.

My colleagues and I witnessed the explosion of incidence of date rape in the mid-1990s, and in the late 1990s it became necessary to make HIV tests mandatory for boys as young as ten, who allegedly raped younger girls! Even secular expert Sigmund Freud would have seen this behavior as aberrant; but today's "sexuality experts", rather than being alarmed, consider this *normal* behavior for 10-year-old boys.

My training as a nurse, and my firsthand experience in STD clinics, caused me to reflect upon the "Christian" sex education I had been taught in Lutheran grade school, the *Learning About Sex* series. Groundbreaking when it was first published, the *Learning About Sex* series had by this time been used in every conservative Christian denomination for going on thirty years.

I found myself having doubts about everything I'd thought was true in this area. It was abundantly clear that the *Learning About Sex* series had *not* produced a standard of purity in my generation. But another factor was making my concerns all the more urgent: In 1997, our oldest son was about to enter a Lutheran school where the *Learning About Sex* series was being taught to the next generation of Christian children. In God's providence, all of the curriculums at the Lutheran schools were under review at that time, and I was chosen to review the *Learning About Sex* series. My role in this process began as a minor one, but I undertook my commission with a peculiar urgency, and what I found absolutely stunned me.

I learned that sex education was an integral part of a much larger plan—the Sexual Revolution.

Revolutions don't just happen overnight, and the Sexual Revolution was no exception; it didn't occur out of nowhere in the 1960s, but began many years before. Furthermore, revolutions don't just happen by themselves; revolutions need revolutionaries, and, again, the Sexual Revolution was no different. Alfred Kinsey and a group called SEICUS were those revolutionaries, who worked *diligently* to bring about their goals. They achieved one of the most devastating revolutions of all time.

Researching sex education was like looking at an iceberg; it may not look so big, but 85% of an iceberg lies below the surface of the water. Sex education was just the tip of a large, mountainous iceberg, with many layers to it.

> Now the Spirit expressly says that in latter times some will depart from the faith, giving heed to deceiving spirits and doctrines of demons, speaking lies in hypocrisy, having their own conscience seared with a hot iron... (1 Timothy 4:1–2)

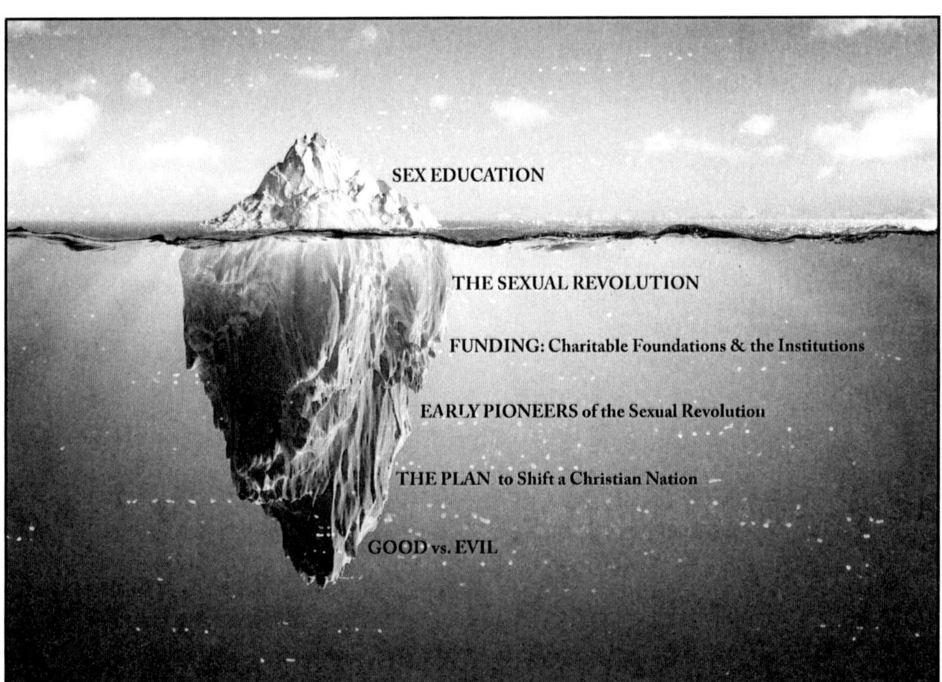


Sex Education was just the tip of the iceberg, an integral part in the plan to bring about the Sexual Revolution.

In order to help you Know Your History, we're going to dive down through the layers of that iceberg. In the rest of this chapter, we'll lay the foundation with the four lowest layers, and in the following chapters we'll take a more detailed look at the history of the Sexual Revolution and, finally, sex education.

As you read, watch for three main themes you'll see woven through this iceberg: Humanism, Communism, and Eugenics. A vast conspiracy, you may ask? No, it is simply a well-orchestrated **revolution**.

## GOOD VS. EVIL

In the beginning God created... (Genesis 1:1)

At the base of the iceberg is a conflict that goes back to the very Beginning. The story of sex education, although it has affected the whole world, largely took place in America. Nevertheless the ultimate schemer in this tale was that old serpent, Satan.

So where does this history start?

God created the first man and woman, Adam and Eve, in His image and likeness. Satan then tempted them through means of deception, and they rebelled against God. But God, in a marvelous display of His grace and mercy, promised a Savior who would come to earth to redeem Adam, Eve, and their descendants from the punishment for their sins.[1]

Centuries later, Adam and Eve's descendants having given themselves over to sin, the world was overtaken by evil and perversity.

Noah sending the dove, from 12th century Venetian mosaic.
(Image credit: Wikimedia Commons.)

[1] Genesis 1–3.

> Then the Lord saw that the wickedness of man was great in the earth, and that every intent of the thoughts of his heart was only evil continually. And the Lord was sorry that He had made man on the earth, and He was grieved in His heart. So the Lord said, "I will destroy man whom I have created from the face of the earth, both man and beast, creeping thing and birds of the air, for I am sorry that I have made them." (Genesis 6:5–7)

But rather than destroy mankind entirely, in his mercy He provided a way of salvation for us yet again, and commissioned Noah, his wife, his sons, and their wives to be the one family surviving God's destruction.[2]

To this day, Satan continues to use the tools of deceit and man's inhumanity toward man to destroy nations. There is nothing new under the sun.[3]

## THE PLAN TO SHIFT A CHRISTIAN NATION

> This book of the law shall not depart out of thy mouth; but thou shalt meditate therein day and night; that thou mayest observe to do according to all that is written therein; for then thou shalt make thy way prosperous, and then thou shalt have good success. (Joshua 1:8)

People trained to identify forgeries are prepared by a thorough study of... not great examples of forgery, but, rather, the real deal. The better they know the authentic item, the better prepared they are to spot a fake.

We are going to be learning to identify some false ideologies that crept into the United States; but why the attack on the United States? Sexual immorality has been a common practice in many nations throughout history; why the great push to transform America? Couldn't the libertines be satisfied to live out their licentiousness in France?

---

[2] Genesis 6–9.

[3] Ecclesiastes 1:9.

The United States of America was unapologetically founded on wisdom and insight from God's Word. We're going to learn that the men behind sex ed embraced counterfeit philosophies... and they were smart enough to realize that their counterfeit philosophies would never stand up under the light of scrutiny if people could compare them against the genuine philosophy of Christianity. (Or if they didn't, their ultimate leader, that old dragon did!)

The United States had been born from humble beginnings, but its foundation was built firmly on the Word of God; and by the 1800s, she was beginning to make waves on the world stage. The gospel message was spreading worldwide, like it had at no time since the days of the Early Church.

America was attacked because America was Christian.

It has become trendy in recent years to name the founding fathers of America who were not committed Christians, and claim that these few examples prove that the founding fathers were not Christians after all.

But the exception proves the rule. It would not be worth noting that Thomas Jefferson and Benjamin Franklin were deists if it weren't that most of the Founding Fathers *were* dedicated Christians. Even in the writings of Franklin and Jefferson, the Christian faith is upheld and put forth as the key to any greatness our nation might have.

William Tyndale, before being strangled and burned at the stake.
(Image credit: Wikimedia Commons.)

During the Reformation, Christians underwent severe persecution across Europe.[4] The French Christians were slaughtered in the St. Bartholomew's Day Massacre; Philip II implemented a campaign of total extermination against the Dutch on account of their faith; in England, Henry VIII and Bloody Mary burned Christians alive. Under the reigns of Queen Elizabeth and her cousin James, imprisonment and all kinds of persecution were carried out against faithful Christians, and the

[4] John Foxe, *Actes and Monuments* (also called *Fox's Book of Martyrs*).

slaughter of innocent men, women, and children was still vivid in Christians' memories.

Under these conditions, faithful Christians fled to the New World, America. They often spent evey penny they had, and many of these Christians died in the harsh realities of this wild and untamed land once they arrived here. But their faith in God and His Word was stronger than their fear of death and poverty. They desired to worship the Lord in obedience to His Word, at any cost.[5]

Not every person who came to America was a Christian, and not every one of those Christians' children grew up to maintain the faith diligently. But many of those who came were of a deeply faithful species of Christian, and the culture of the American colonies that they created was a culture of faithful biblical Christianity.

When the British began to extend their tyranny over the American colonies, the independent United States of America was created by the people of that culture. Many of them—men such as George Washington,

The Mayflower at Sea, author unknown.
(Image credit: Wikimedia Commons.)

[5] William Bradford, *Of Plymouth Plantation: Bradford's History of the Plymouth Settlement 1608–1650* (San Antonio: The Vision Forum, 1998).

Patrick Henry, and Samuel Adams—were true, Holy Spirit-filled disciples of Jesus Christ.[6] Adams, for example—without whom we probably would never have declared independence—believed that tyranny was from "the devil, who is a tyrant, and the father of tyrants and of liars."[7] Freedom, on the other hand, was something worth fighting for because it was a right given by God:

Samuel Adams.
(Image credit: Wikimedia Commons.)

> The right to freedom being the gift of God Almighty, it is not in the power of man to alienate this gift and voluntarily become a slave... [The rights of the colonists] may be best understood by reading and carefully studying the institutes of the great Law Giver and Head of the Christian Church, which are to be found clearly written and promulgated in the New Testament.[8]

The values set forth in our founding documents—the Declaration of Independence, the U.S. Constitution, and the Bill of Rights—strongly reflect biblical principles. America has been referred to as a Christian nation not because she had more Christians or churches, but because her laws and government were founded on the principles of the Old and New Testaments.[9]

Our founders' first laws relied on principles found in the Ten Commandments, which God gave Moses on Mt. Sinai.[10] The Supreme Court, in the *Church of the Holy Trinity v. United States* ruling, authored by Justice David J. Brewer in 1892, stated,

---

[6] Kevin Swanson, *American Faith: 27 Sketches from Winthrop to Wilkerson* (Parker, CO: Generations, 2019), 164–166, 185–187, 198–199, 209–213, 241–243, 247–249.

[7] Kevin Swanson, *American Faith: 27 Sketches from Winthrop to Wilkerson* (Parker, CO: Generations, 2019), 199.

[8] Kevin Swanson, *American Faith: 27 Sketches from Winthrop to Wilkerson* (Parker, CO: Generations, 2019), 199.

[9] David Barton, Wallbuilders, wallbuilders.com.

[10] Exodus 20:1–17.

> From the discovery of this continent to the present hour, there is a single voice making this affirmation... we find everywhere a clear recognition of the same truth... this is a Christian nation.[11]

Over the course of our nation's history, the Supreme Court—on four separate occasions—has ruled that America is a Christian nation; not once have those decisions been overturned.[12]

Why is this important as you begin to learn the hidden story behind the Sexual Revolution? Although America was founded on the principles of the Old and New Testaments, in other nations certain philosophies in opposition to Christianity were becoming influential—the philosophies of humanism, communism, and eugenics.

> For the wisdom of this world is foolishness with God. For it is written, "He catches the wise in their own craftiness," and again, "The Lord knows the thoughts of the wise, that they are futile." (1 Corinthians 3:19–20)

**Humanism** is the rejection of God and His Word; this philosophy teaches that man can make up his own moral rules. Ultimately, humanism is simply a religion which takes God off of the throne of the universe and places humans in that place.

**Communism** is a political system in which a small group rules over the masses with their own interpretation of laws, producing restriction on freedoms. One of the primary tenets of communism is that private property is abolished; in lieu of individuals owning their own property, the government owns everything and claims to know what is best for each person. Like humanism, communism is a religion which places humans in the place of God; however, communism is a specific form of humanism: Instead of claiming that each human is his own god, in communism only the humans running the government are in the place of God, and all of the

---

[11] *Church of the Holy Trinity v. United States* (1892).

[12] There are four separate decisions of the U.S. Supreme Court which assert that the United States is—in law, fact, and history—and should thus properly be termed officially a "Christian Nation", because of the foundation of our laws upon principles of the Ten Commandments, and the Old and New Testaments. Those Court decisions are *Vidal v. Girard's Executors* (1844) [cited in *Marsh v. Chambers* and *Abinton v. Schempp*]; *Mormon Church v. United States* (1889) [also cited in *Abington v. Schempp*]; *Church of the Holy Trinity v. United States* (1892); and *U.S. v. MacIntosh* (1931).

other people must recognize that the government owns everything and knows what is best.

**Eugenics** is the elimination of an entire group of people. Famously, Margaret Sanger's work to "eliminate" African Americans and Adolf Hitler's efforts to "eliminate" the Jews were the result of their faith in eugenics. This humanist philosophy comes from the Darwinian idea that humans are not all of one race descended from Adam and Eve (the human race), but that humans are of difference races, as different as monkeys are from gorillas, and that, for the betterment of humanity as a whole, the "less evolved" races should no longer be permitted to "breed".

As famously alluded to by founding fathers John Adams and James Madison, even if you are not a Christian, it is always to your benefit to live in a Christian nation where liberty and freedom would be secure.

In the production of his movie *Monumental: In Search of America's National Treasure*, Christian father and concerned citizen Kirk Cameron was led to the National Monument to the Forefathers, in Plymouth, Massachusetts. This monument, completed in 1889, was erected to remind future generations—lest we forget—what it was that made America great. It is comprised of five large statues. The largest stands in the middle of this monument, holding a Bible and pointing to the heavens. The four statues surrounding her are Morality, Law, Education, and Liberty. All four of these lesser statues revolve around the centerpiece, which is Faith.

A country with its foundation on God and His Word, whose goal was to have biblical Morality be the Law of the land, also had Education and Liberty proceed out of this biblical foundation.

In the face of this strength, Satan deployed an old tactic, one which he has used successfully many times throughout history to destroy men and nations—the vehicle of sexual immorality. The Sexual Revolution was designed to rid this nation of its biblical morality. A people who embrace sin must abandon the Christian faith.

And if you can remove the foundation, the entire structure will fall.

# EARLY PIONEERS OF THE SEXUAL REVOLUTION

> See to it that no one takes you captive through hollow and deceptive philosophy, which depends on human tradition and the basic principles of this world rather than on Christ.
> (Colossians 2:8, NIV)

A few people—some names familiar, some not—had outsized roles in this tale of treachery. We'll go into more detail about how the Sexual Revolution came about in the next chapter, but for now, familiarize yourself with these names:

Charles Darwin.
(Image credit: Wikimedia Commons.)

**Charles Darwin** (1809–1882). In the late 1700s and early 1800s, humanism, arising out of France, became a popular philosophy in Great Britain and, increasingly, in the United States, in a movement called The Enlightenment. In 1859, Charles Darwin published *On the Origin of Species*, in which he claimed to have scientific evidence that animals, man, and all other life were not created by God supernaturally in six days, but that they had all evolved from one initial bunch of molecules, initially jolted into life by a random natural occurence. Many of the elites in the Western world quickly embraced this thin façade of "scientific reasoning" as a way to excuse themselves from any allegiance to God or duty to obey his law. Before, apostates were kept back from a complete denial of God and his Christ by the ultimate fear of Hell; now, they threw off His "shackles" entirely. This trickled down to the rest of our society through the schools; Creation was rejected in the schools, and Evolution went from being taught to children as a theory, to being taught as Science.

> Why do... the people plot a vain thing... against the Lord and against His Anointed, saying, "Let us break Their bonds in pieces and cast away Their cords from us." He who sits in the heavens shall laugh... (Psalm 2:1–4)

**Thomas Huxley** (1825–1895). Known as "Darwin's Bulldog", Huxley gave public lectures and wrote in support of Darwin's theory; he played an important role in bringing Darwin's ideas into wide acceptance. Huxley coined the term "agnostic", meaning a person who claims neither faith nor disbelief in God. His grandsons, Aldous and Julian Huxley, were instrumental players in the Sexual Revolution. If Aldous Huxley's name sounds familiar, it's because he was the author of the dsytopian novel *Brave New World*.

Thomas Huxley was known as Darwin's Bulldog.
(Image credit: Wikimedia Commons.)

Sigmund Freud created what he called the stages of psychosexual development.
(Image credit: Wikimedia Commons.)

**Sigmund Freud** (1856–1939). Influenced by Darwin and Huxley, Freud was an evolutionist and an atheist. In essence, he created a plan of salvation for lost souls in the religion of humanism—psychotherapy, which developed into the modern fields of psychiatry and psychology. He considered the questions, *If there is no God, then there is no sin. But if there is no sin, how do we deal with murder, theft, adultery, and other problems? The Christian religion had taught that men have a sinful nature, but now that we've "proven" that Christianity is false, how do we explain why some people choose these behaviors? And what do we call these behaviors that we think aren't good, if there's no such thing as sin?* Freud rejected the idea of man's sinful nature and promoted the premise that man is not responsible for what he does, but that someone else is. Sin was no longer called sin, but a disorder. In Christianity, man is absolutely powerless to save himself from his own sins, thus he needs

One greater than himself to save him. But in psychology, man *suffers* from disordered thinking, or a bad environment, and if he can receive the right counseling, he can free himself (save himself) from his *disorders*. Freud developed the five stages of psychosexual development based on his philosophy, which laid the groundwork for the Sexual Revolution.

John Dewey.
Image credit: Wikimedia Commons.)

**John Dewey** (1859–1952). Dewey was a sociologist influenced by the theories of Darwin. He wanted to show that the evolution of the species could be applied to human sociology and education. One result of Dewey's influence was the elimination of the one-room schoolhouse; he divided schools into grade levels based on students' ages in the misguided belief that, in childhood, humans relive their evolutionary ancestry; therefore, an eight-year-old should no more be in the same classroom with a six-year-old than Neanderthal Man should be in the same classroom with Piltdown Man. He helped develop the public school education system based on Progressive Era ideas about social reform and pragmatism. A signer of the Humanist Manifesto and a socialist, he mocked biblical authority and believed that only man's authority could be relied upon.

**Margaret Sanger** (1879–1966). Devoted to the cause of birth control, Sanger was a sex educator, eugenicist, member of the socialist party, and the founder of the world's largest abortion provider, Planned Parenthood International. In a 1939 letter about her "Negro Project", she wrote, "We don't want the word to go out that we want to exterminate the Negro population..." In her 1920 book *Woman and the New Race*, she wrote, "The most merciful thing that the large family does to one of its infant members is to kill it." She had many adulterous relationships, including with fellow progressive and author H.G. Wells, who was himself a student of Thomas Huxley.

Margaret Sanger.
(Image credit: Wikimedia Commons.)

**Alfred Kinsey** (1894–1956). Considered the father of the Sexual Revolution, Kinsey's famous "studies" suggested that children ought to be pleasure seekers, and proclaimed that "children are sexual from birth." He concluded that there should be no limits to any sexual activity and was instrumental in revisions to the Sex Offence sections of law codes in most states and across the world.[13]

Alfred Kinsey.
(Image credit: Wikimedia Commons.)

His most well-known disciples included:

- Hugh Hefner, founder of the pornography industry.
- Harry Hay, founder of the Gay Civil Rights movement and supporter of NAMBLA (North American Man Boy Love Association).
- William Masters, best known from the Masters and Johnson sexuality research team.
- John Money, who provided the foundation for the transgender movement today.
- Alan Guttmacher, founder of Planned Parenthood's Guttmacher Institute.[14]

[13] Judith Reisman, Ph.D.; Dennis Jerrard, Ph.D.; Colonel Ronald Ray U.S.M.C.; & Eunice Ray; *RSVP America Training Manual* (Crestwood, KY: First Principles, Inc., 1996), 1–30.

[14] For more information, see the British Documentary "Secret History: Kinsey's Pedophiles," on YouTube, available at rsvpamerica.org, or drjudithreisman.org.

# FUNDING: CHARITABLE FOUNDATIONS & THE INSTITUTIONS

To what were its foundations fastened? Or who laid its cornerstone? (Judges 17:6)

The charitable foundations and large institutions of the twentieth century were a crucial force in ushering God, morality, and the knowledge of our social framework out of American thought.

They welcomed in faux science and social neutralization, in which it was argued that just because people view something as wrong, doesn't mean it *is* wrong. (Ever heard of "values-neutral" instruction? Yep, that's it.)

The foundations and institutions were some of the most powerful forces at work during the Progressive Era (and are to this day).

In 1913, for the first time in United States history, an income tax was laid upon Americans, a gift the Progressive Era left us. Except... for certain "charitable" organizations, which were granted tax exemption in the very law that established the income tax.[15] John D. Rockefeller, Andrew Carnegie, and Henry Ford were making unthinkable amounts of wealth with the explosion of industrialization; and the bulk of their money would be protected from taxation if they funnelled it into tax-exempt foundations. They simply had to use the money to "do good". With men like Darwin, Huxley, and Freud redefining Good and Evil according to their humanist ideas, and the income tax forcing the industrialists to channel as much of their money as possible into foundations for doing "good", what could go wrong?

The tax-exempt foundations of Rockefeller, Carnegie, and Ford were used to fund the Sexual Revolution; through their foundations, these men worked outside of the democratic process to reshape society. Here are some selected highlights of what these foundations accomplished in relation to the Sexual Revolution.

---

[15] Paul Arnsberger, Melissa Ludlum, Margaret Riley, and Mark Stanton, "A History of the Tax-Exempt Sector: An SOI Perspective," https://www.irs.gov/pub/irs-soi/tehistory.pdf.

Andrew Carnegie, John D. Rockefeller with his son John Jr., Henry Ford.
(Image credits: Wikimedia Commons.)

In **1910**, the Carnegie Foundation paid for a study of American medical schools; more than anything else, the study was critical of instruction in the field of obstetrics. In response to the study's finding, the foundation gave large grants to medical schools that moved away from teaching naturopathy, homeopathy, and chiropractic in favor of medicine based on surgery and the emerging field of pharmacology. Birth control became a focal point in obstetric medicine.

Since the time of Marx, eager Marxists had long worked to create a church group spanning denominational differences that would promote socialism within the church. This group, the Federal Council of Churches, was successfully established in 1908, and by 1914 it was fulfilling its objectives quite well. In **1914**, leaders of the FCC met at Andrew Carnegie's home, and formed a "controlling group" within the FCC, which was fully funded by him. (Fun fact: Today, the Federal Council of Churches is called the National Council of Churches.)

In **1918**, Carnegie endowed the American Historical Association to rewrite American history. All references to God and His divine providence were removed from the history books for children.

In **1923**, Carnegie endowed the American Bar Association's "American Law Institute" (ALI). You're going to hear a lot more about the ALI as this book goes on, so you might as well learn that name now. The ALI targeted fifty-two laws that protected marriage, women, and children to be removed.

In the same year, **1923**, John D. Rockefeller not only funded the ALI, but Margaret Sanger and her eugenic vision. (Now do you see why I used scare quotes when I tell you about the federal requirement that tax-exempt organizations "do good"?)

From **1941–1949**, *the Rockefeller Foundation funded Alfred Kinsey's sex studies.* I know you don't understand the full implications of that yet, but I'm drawing your attention to this now anyway; you'll learn more about it in the next chapter.

Concerned over the shifting social structure in America, in **1951** Congressman E. E. Cox introduced a resolution to the U.S. House of Representatives to direct a thorough investigation of the tax-exempt foundations, and the resolution passed the full House the following year.[16]

He specifically named the Rockefeller Foundation,

> Whose funds have been used to finance individuals and organizations whose business it has been to get communism into the private and public schools of the country...[17]

Rene Wormser, legal counsel to the Reece Committee (which followed the Cox Committee) later reported,

> The Cox Committee did find that there had been a Communist Moscow-directed plot to infiltrate American foundations and to use their funds for Communist purposes, but they reported that they had felt hurried by the lack of time to sufficiently investigate further.[18]

Do you remember the American Law Institute? In **1952**, the same year that the Cox Committee began to investigate the tax-exempt foundations, the ALI undertook a major project they named the Model Penal Code. In it, "model laws" were written, which the states and federal government would be encouraged to use as models for revising the existing, Bible-based laws. As their authority on what is normal sexuality, the Model Penal Code looked to Alfred Kinsey—who suggested that adult-child "sex" (that would be rape, by a pedophile) is healthy, and that rape itself

---

[16] For more information, see the British Documentary "Secret History: Kinsey's Pedophiles," on YouTube, available at rsvpamerica.org, or drjudithreisman.org.

[17] Rene A. Wormser, *Foundations: Their Power and Influence* (New York: The Devin-Adair Company, 1958), vii–xiii.

[18] Ibid. (p. 348–382).

is a myth because sexual activity is always beneficial for any "partner".[19] Rather than punish rapists and pedophiles, the Model Penal Code prescribed therapy for offenders. In the next few decades, Model Penal Code laws were quickly adopted by state after state. The Rockefeller Foundation funded this project.

In **1952**, John D. Rockefeller III (son of John Jr. and grandson of John) established The Population Council to look at population control. Fred Osburn, President of the Eugenics Society, ran the day-to-day operations.[20] Yes, seven years after pictures of the Nazi concentration camps came out and shocked the world—and proved the death-knell for the open use of the *word* Eugenics—these guys were still diligently creating new venues for their eugenic efforts. They were true believers.

B. Carol Reece.
(Image credit: Wikimedia Commons.)

Remember the Cox Committee? What they found raised some eyebrows. The following year, in **1953**, Congressman B. Carol Reece introduced another resolution to investigate the foundations further; again, this resolution was passed by the full House. The Reece Committee focused particularly on the funding that the foundations were providing in the fields of the social sciences, education, and international affairs. (Note that in the phrase "social sciences", the operative word is *social*, not *science*. Science means *knowledge* about something; the social sciences are fields for the purpose of gaining knowledge about *society*—people.) The Reece Committee looked specifically into the Rockefeller-Kinsey connection and stated that this was a deliberate attack on Judeo-Christian morality.[21]

---

[19] Linda Jeffrey, Ed.D. & Colonel Ronald D. Ray, J.D., *A History of the American Law Institute's Model Penal Code: The Kinsey Reports' Influence on "Science-based" Legal Reform 1923–2007* (Crestwood, KY: First Principles, Inc., 2007).

[20] Linda Jeffrey, Ed.D., "Why Not Indulge? The Health Implications: Exploring the History and Research of Chemicals Altering Women's Natural Hormone System" (Crestwood, KY: First Principles, Inc., 2005, available at matthewxviii.org/articles).

[21] Rene A. Wormser, *Foundations: Their Power and Influence* (New York: The Devin-Adair Company, 1958), 348–382.

In **1954**, the Reece Committee had the task of telling the taxpayer that:

> [T]he incredible was, in fact, truth... That the huge fortunes piled up by such industrial giants as John D. Rockefeller, Andrew Carnegie, and Henry Ford were today being used to destroy or discredit the free-enterprise system which gave them birth.[22]

In **1957**, Illinois became the first state to adopt the Model Penal Code (based on Kinsey's "science") in the Sex Offense section of their laws, throwing out laws on morality that were based on the Bible. The Illinois Commission stated why it was important to embrace Kinsey's propaganda that, "Children are sexual from birth:"

> Children of our times are inadequately trained to live in a free society. The inability of some parents to rear children in a democratic atmosphere and, at the same time, to observe the conventions of society is a fact that needs consideration... [Crime] Prevention through mental hygiene and sex education for both adults and children may prove to be effective. Sex education is more than information about physiological functions; it must consider the more subtle emotional attitude toward both sexes and their relationship to one another.[23]

Every other state followed suit, within the next thirty years.

Most of the fifty-two laws that protected marriage, women, and chidren which the ALI originally targeted for removal back in 1923 have been removed, as of 2020. For example, laws against rape were weakened to make it very difficult for men to be convicted of the crime, and laws against pornography were removed.[24]

As you read on now about the Sexual Revolution and sex ed, keep in mind the four levels that supported them—the age-old battle of Good vs. Evil, the deliberate plan to shift a Christian nation, the early pioneers of these ideas, and the funding and institutions that made it all possible. They undergirded everything that was to come.

---

[22] Ibid., vii.

[23] O. Richardson, *Missouri Law Review*, Vol. 38 (1973), 397.

[24] Linda Jeffrey, Ed.D. & Colonel Ronald D. Ray, J.D., *A History of the American Law Institute's Model Penal Code: The Kinsey Reports' Influence on "Science-based" Legal Reform 1923–2007* (Crestwood, KY: First Principles, Inc., 2007), 35.

Chapter 2

# The Sexual Revolution: Early History

The fool hath said, in his heart, there is no God. They are corrupt, they have done abominable works, there is none that doeth good. (Psalm 14:1, KJV)

Do you think that the Sexual Revolution occurred in 1967 with the "Summer of Love"? Think again.

The goals of the Sexual Revolution were laid out by Marxists during the late 1800s through the early 1900s, and these revolutionaries labored diligently to bring their vision to pass in the Western world. Then, after Alfred Kinsey published his infamous book in 1948, the revolutionaries claimed the mantle of "science" for their ideas; and only two short decades later, the "Sexual Revolution" was announced out in the open as societal fact.

From the 1800s to the present, the trail runs: Quietly, the ideas were shared in progressive circles; deceptively, societal changes were sold to church leaders and society at large; intentionally, committed followers of these ideas worked their way into leadership positions in educational and media institutions... until enough ground had been gained that the revolutionaries felt confident enough to declare their revolution openly.

We only saw their victory dance in the Summer of Love.

*The Sexual Revolution began well before the 1960s.*

Now that you know a bit about the lower layers of the iceberg, it's time to tell the story of the Sexual Revolution. In this chapter we'll look at the early history through the publication of Kinsey's book, and in the next we'll see what happened in the wake of that event.[1]

## THE LANDS OF LUTHER AND THE REFORMATION

> "The servants said to him, 'Do you want us then to go and gather [the tares] up?' But he said, 'No, lest while you gather up the tares you also uproot the wheat with them. Let both grow together until the harvest, and at the time of harvest I will say to the reapers, "First gather together the tares and bind them in bundles to burn them, but gather the wheat into my barn."'" (Matthew 13:28–30)

You'll remember that in the late 1700s, humanism coming out of France began to spread to the United States, England, and other European countries. We think of those nations as being Christian lands in those days—and in the culture at large, as well as in those nations' laws, they were. But there will always be nonbelievers, even in the most wonderful Christian churches or lands. The story of the Sexual Revolution begins in the countries of Luther, John Bunyan, and the Pilgrims... with a few men who wanted none of it.

---

[1] Unless otherwise noted, the facts in the next three chapters are taken from five books:

- Judith Reisman, Ph.D.; Dennis Jerrard, Ph.D.; Colonel Ronald Ray U.S.M.C.; & Eunice Ray; *RSVP America Training Manual* (Crestwood, KY: First Principles, Inc., 1996).
- Judith Reisman, PhD, *Kinsey, Crimes and Consequences* (Crestwood, KY: The Institute for Media Education, 2000).
- Claire Chambers, *The SIECUS Circle: A Humanist Revolution* (Belmont, MA: Western Islands, 1977).
- Randy Engel, *Sex Education: The Final Plague* (Gaithersburg, MD: Human Life International, 1989).
- Karen Booth, *Forgetting How To Blush: United Methodism's Compromise with the Sexual Revolution* (Fort Valley, GA: Bristol House, Ltd., 2012).

The publication of Darwin's book gave men who resented the laws of God all the excuse they needed to throw off biblical morality entirely. England—the land of William Tyndale, John Bunyan, and the Puritans—now became an exporter of atheism and agnosticism.

The same year that Darwin published *On the Origin of Species*, another book was published in Germany. The lazy son of a staggeringly wealthy lawyer, who had run through his entire inheritance via prodigal living—such that three of his children died of malnutrition while he kept up his own pleasures...[2] In Germany, this man whose name was Karl Marx published *The Communist Manifesto*.

In 1859, Karl Marx published *The Communist Manifesto*.
(Image credit: Wikimedia Commons.)

Those who embraced Marx's anti-Christian ideas were called communists, socialists, Nazis—or, for simplicity's sake, Marxists. Marxists were committed to transforming their Christian countries into humanist "Utopias". They believed they were leading Progress from their apish ancestry to the point—soon to be realized—when humans would attain their rightful status as gods, directing their own destiny.

The Marxists understood that temptation to sexual sin would be a powerful motivator to lead Christians out of the churches, so they intentionally pushed for the acceptance—and even embrace—of sexual immorality in our culture and laws. But they had an even bigger motivation to fight for the rejection of God's standards for morality in our culture: These folks were immoral, themselves. They didn't like the dispproval and difficulty they faced from society at large for their adulteries and other immoralities.

---

[2] James Simpson, *Who Was Karl Marx? The Men, the Motives, and the Menace Behind Today's Rampaging American Left* (Baltimore, MD: Simpson Publishing, 2021), 7–10; or watch interview with Curtis Bowers at https://rumble.com/vk8vna-karl-marx-the-father-of-critical-race-theory-curtis-bowers.html.

In the later 1800s through around 1933, Germany—the land of Luther, the *Ninety-Five Theses*, and the Reformation—became a mecca for pansexual and homosexual activity. Hundreds of cabarets in Berlin were havens for all kinds of sexual immorality, and homosexual bars were a thriving part of this licentious culture. Intellectuals wrote philosophically in support of sodomy and cross-dressing; organizations were formed to advocate for homosexual "rights"; publications and entertainment featured not-so-thinly veiled encouragement to this sort of behavior. In 1919, the film *Different from the Others* was the story of a man who struggled with his homosexuality, and by 1931 it wasn't veiled at all when *Mädchen in Uniform* sympathetically told the tale of the lead character's lesbian "love" (lust) for her teacher. In Berlin, the Institute for Sexual Science encouraged cross-dressing and performed transgender surgeries.

Dr. Magnus Hirschfeld founded the Institute for Sexual Science in 1919.
(Image credit: Wikimedia Commons.)

Hirschfeld himself played the doctor in the film *Different from the Others*.
(Image credit: Wikimedia Commons.)

In 1921, the first International Congress for Sexual Reform met in Berlin. They determined to pursue:

- Repeal of laws making sodomy a crime.
- Legalization of prostitution.
- Legalization and promotion of contraception techniques.
- Establishment of sexual counseling centers (such as Planned Parenthood clinics).
- "Liberation" of marriage (i.e., expansion of grounds for divorce).
- Repeal of laws against abortion (baby killing).
- Repeal of laws against obscenity (pornography and sex education).
- Sex education for youth and adults.

*Science and Invention for January*

Mrs. Margaret Sanger, the great birth control advocate, and her two sons

**"WOMAN AND THE NEW RACE"**

**By Margaret Sanger**

This book, just published, is Margaret Sanger's greatest effort for the birth control movement. It contains the very essence of her life's work. It instructs the women of the world in the greatest step of their emancipation. "WOMAN AND THE NEW RACE" contains the sum total of Margaret Sanger's experience and knowledge on this vital subject—knowledge she dared to utter and print—knowledge for which she faced jail and fought through every court to establish as woman's inalienable right.

**PART OF CONTENTS**

| | |
|---|---|
| Woman's Error and her Debt | Continence: Is it Practicable or Desirable? |
| The Struggle for Freedom | Contraception or Abortion? |
| Two Classes of Women | Are Preventive Means Certain? |
| Immorality of Unwanted Large Families | Battalion of Unwanted Babies Cause of War |
| Cries of Despair | Woman and Morality |
| Women who plead for Abortion | Legislating Woman's Morals |
| When should a Woman avoid having children? | Why not Birth Control Clinics in America? |

Any one chapter is worth the price of this book

**THE KNOWLEDGE IS PRICELESS**

This book, "Woman and the New Race," by Margaret Sanger, contains so much that is vital, thorough and necessary to every married couple, that it would require a book to describe it. THE KNOWLEDGE OF BIRTH CONTROL WILL BRING HAPPINESS TO EVERY MARRIAGE.

Price Only $2.00 Sent Prepaid

Order at Once. Don't Delay.

**TRUTH PUBLISHING CO.**

1400 Broadway Dept. 5-G New York

Margaret Sanger promoted birth control, abortion, and the "elimination" of entire classes of people.

(Image credit: Wikimedia Commons.)

In America—the land of the Pilgrims, Jonathan Edwards, and the Founding Fathers—during the late 1800s and early 1900s the wealthy elite were instituting the planks of the Communist Manifesto as fast as they could. This period in American history is labeled—by historians who approved of Marxism—the Progressive Era.

The average church-going American was blissfully unaware of the true views of the people who were publishing all of the new books and newspapers, and running the industrial monopolies which were transforming daily life. But out of the view of the average person, the progressives were hard at work to transform our Christian society into a communist, humanist one. They worked at their goals with more or less stealth, depending on what tactic seemed best to suit their purposes at the time.

In 1921, Margaret Sanger founded the Birth Control League, which would later be renamed Planned Parenthood. She wrote numerous articles and books, spoke across the country, met with leaders of different communities—you will be especially interested to know that she intentionally appealed to churches, teaching pastors to teach their congregations to use methods to prevent conception and birth—and worked tirelessly her entire life to eliminate as many people as she possibly could before they were even born. Before they were even *conceived*.

Sanger was the founder and editor-in-chief of the *Birth Control Review*.
(Image credit: Wikimedia Commons.)

We touched on this in the previous chapter, but we cannot move on without reiterating that Sanger was unapologetically working to see the entire African American population "exterminated" through convincing their people to stop "breeding", the term she almost exclusively used to speak of bearing children. She advocated for the forcible sterilization of the diabled and other people she deemed "unfit to breed"—you know, like people who were poor. She claimed to be a Christian only to gain entry into protestant Christian circles, where her views came to be embraced.

Aldous Huxley's *Brave New World* is a suicidal, godless tale.
(Image credit: Wikimedia Commons.)

Across the pond, an Englishman was making a noteworthy contribution to our history of the Sexual Revolution. In 1932, Aldous Huxley published *Brave New World*. You will remember that Aldous' grandfather Thomas, Darwin's Bulldog, was the man who famously coined the term *agnostic*. *Brave New World* was a dystopian novel which suggested that children engage in sexual activities in the classroom and imagined a state-run fertility program, complete with artificial wombs and eugenic planning. This immoral story was presented as science fiction, but in actuality it was written to cast a vision for America in the future.

In Germany during the early-to-mid 1930s, Adolf Hitler and the Nazis were increasingly consolidating the power they'd won through popular election into absolute tyranny. Seeing the communists as political rivals to crush, the nazis began arresting them. (Communists fight for international socialism; the nazis fought for national socialism.) The thing that was noteworthy about that was that quite a few of the Marxists and sexual libertines who fled Berlin during that period immigrated to the United States in the 1930s.

## KINSEY'S SEX STUDIES

> Professing to be wise, they became fools... Therefore God also gave them up to uncleanness, in the lusts of their hearts, to dishonor their bodies among themselves... God gave them up to vile passions. For even their women exchanged the natural use for what is against nature. Likewise also the men, leaving the natural use of the woman, burned in their lust for one another, men with men committing what is shameful... (Romans 1:22-27)

In 1938, five years after the closure of the Institute for Sexual Science in Berlin, the same year that Hitler successfully invaded Czechoslovakia, Alfred Kinsey began "studying" "human sexuality" at Indiana University under the guise of a "Marriage Class".

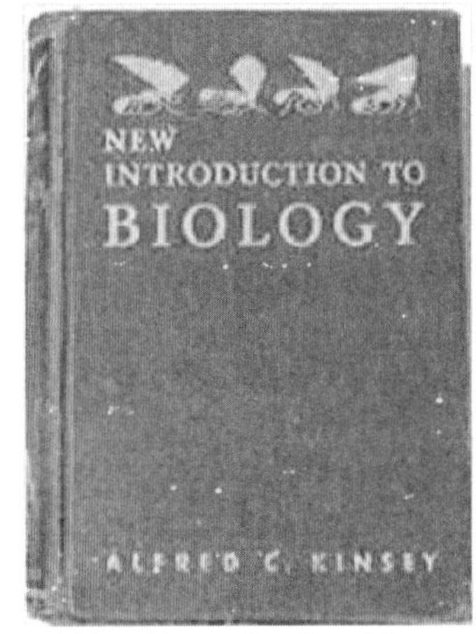

Kinsey wrote the first Biology textbook teaching Darwinism..
(Image credit: Wikimedia Commons.)

Alfred Kinsey was a professor of zoology. He had established his scientific credentials by studying the sexual behavior of the gall wasp and authoring a biology textbook which was groundbreaking for its claims that Darwinian evolutionary theory was true, and views to the contrary nonsensical.

Kinsey (center) with the staff of the Institute for Sexual Research, later renamed with Kinsey Institute.
(Image credit: Wikimedia Commons.)

As a Darwinist, Kinsey saw humans as just another animal, which ought to be studied with the same dispassionate scientific scrutiny with which modern scientists studied animals or insects.

French and German sources being translated, at Kinsey Institute library.
(Image credit: Wikimedia Commons.)

Kinsey's sex studies on humans at Indiana University began with the first "Marriage Class" to college students, which became the first human sexuality course to be taught in American colleges. In 1941, the Rockefeller Foundation granted him funding for these sexuality "studies", and in 1942, he founded the Institute for Sex Research.

In 1948, he published his findings in *Sexual Behavior in the Human Male*, and the book was immediately lauded and promoted by the media and academic elites.

Kinsey's book claimed to have proven what was normal human sexuality in men—that 85% of American men commit fornication before marriage (in the 1940s!), that nearly 70% of American men engage in sex with prostitutes, that 30–45% of husbands commit adultery, and that up to 37% of the adult male population have had homosexual experiences.

The research (supposedly) showed that all forms of sodomy are natural and healthy, that all sexual expression is healthy for individuals (whether pedophilia, incest, bestiality, sodomy, or any other perversion), that early masturbation is critical for good health, etc., etc. Kinsey taught that, "As the aim of coitus is orgasm, the more orgasms from any 'outlet', at the earliest age, the healthier the person."[3] Kinsey claimed to have arrived at these conclusions by interviewing thousands of American men.

The book declared that, in light of these scientific findings, all cultural and religious taboos against these "natural" and "healthy" behaviors were harmful to all of the people who secretly had all of these "normal" desires.

However, in actuality, most of the men Kinsey interviewed for his studies were sexually deviant criminals in prison. Remember, where were most of the average American men during the 1940s? In Europe or the South Pacific fighting in World War II! Even of the few normal men who were not serving overseas, Kinsey did not go into the churches to find voluteers for his studies; again, he went to the prisons.

| AGE | NO. OF ORGASMS | TIME INVOLVED | AGE | NO. OF ORGASMS | TIME INVOLVED |
|---|---|---|---|---|---|
| 5 mon. | 3 | ? | 11 yr. | 11 | 1 hr. |
| 11 mon. | 10 | 1 hr. | 11 yr. | 19 | 1 hr. |
| 11 mon. | 14 | 38 min. | 12 yr. | 7 | 3 hr. |
| 2 yr. | 7 | 9 min. | 12 yr. | 3 | 3 min. |
| | 11 | 65 min. | | 9 | 2 hr. |
| 2½ yr. | 4 | 2 min. | 12 yr. | 12 | 2 hr. |
| 4 yr. | 6 | 5 min. | 12 yr. | 15 | 1 hr. |
| 4 yr. | 17 | 10 hr. | 13 yr. | 7 | 24 min. |
| 4 yr. | 26 | 24 hr. | 13 yr. | 8 | 2½ hr. |
| 7 yr. | 7 | 3 hr. | 13 yr. | 9 | 8 hr. |
| 8 yr. | 8 | 2 hr. | | 3 | 70 sec. |
| 9 yr. | 7 | 68 min. | 13 yr. | 11 | 8 hr. |
| 10 yr. | 9 | 52 min. | | 26 | 24 hr. |
| 10 yr. | 14 | 24 hr. | 14 yr. | 11 | 4 hr. |

**Table 34. Examples of multiple orgasm in pre-adolescent males**

Table 34, from *Sexual Behavior in the Human Male.*

(Image credit: Wikimedia Commons.)

Even more shocking is the data not taken from interviews, but from actual "experimentation".

For the childhood data, Kinsey interviewed pedophiles who "studied" children, using stopwatches, sometimes even making use of the soundproofed rooms at the Institute itself. Kinsey's description of preadolescent "orgasm" included "groaning, sobbing, or more violent cries... will fight away from the partner." The book contains four charts of "data" describing the results of these "studies" on children.

[3] Judith Reisman, PhD, *Kinsey, Crimes and Consequences* (Crestwood, KY: The Institute for Media Education, 2000), 169.

Based on this supposedly scientific research, Kinsey concluded that, "All children are sexual from birth." He claimed that children needed sexual experience from the earliest age for good physical, psychological, and mental health. Therefore, for the good of children, there should be no prohibitions on incest or adult-child sex (again, rape). Because children had these "natural" and "healthy" sexual "needs", they should be sexualized as early as possible.

But the glowing priase of the media and academic elites never mentioned that Kinsey himself was a homosexual and a pedophile. He had an agenda from the very start of his "studies". As for his researchers, Kinsey required the staff of the Kinsey Institute—and their wives—to participate in his perverted "research" as a condition of employment.[4]

Just like with Darwin's book 89 years earlier, Kinsey's book was quickly accepted by academic and cultural leaders in the West as Truth because it claimed to be Science. The impact was immediate, and dramatic.

When I learned about Alfred Kinsey and the origins of the Sexual Revolution... When I thought I would despair at how powerful these evil forces had been to wreak destruction and havoc in the lives of so many people, I remembered this parable:

> Therefore whoever hears these sayings of Mine, and does them, I will liken him to a wise man who built his house on the rock: and the rain descended, the floods came, and the winds blew and beat on that house; and it did not fall, for it was founded on the rock. But everyone who hears these sayings of Mine, and does not do them, will be like a foolish man who built his house on the sand: and the rain descended, the floods came, and the winds blew and beat on that house; and it fell. And great was its fall. (Matthew 7:24–27)

These guys built on sand.

---

[4] Judith Reisman, PhD, *Kinsey, Crimes and Consequences* (Crestwood, KY: The Institute for Media Education, 2000), 74.

Chapter 3

# The Sexual Revolution: Later History

And have no fellowship with the unfruitful works of darkness, but rather expose them. (Ephesians 5:11)

The publication of Kinsey's *Sexual Behavior in the Human Male* was like the opening of the floodgates. Newspapers nationwide immediately published Kinsey's findings as scientific Fact. If anyone was asking for a second opinion, their voices were silenced by the propaganda machine of radio, newsprint, and motion pictures, which had been perfected during World War II. Then, the new invention of the television ushered all of this into every American living room.

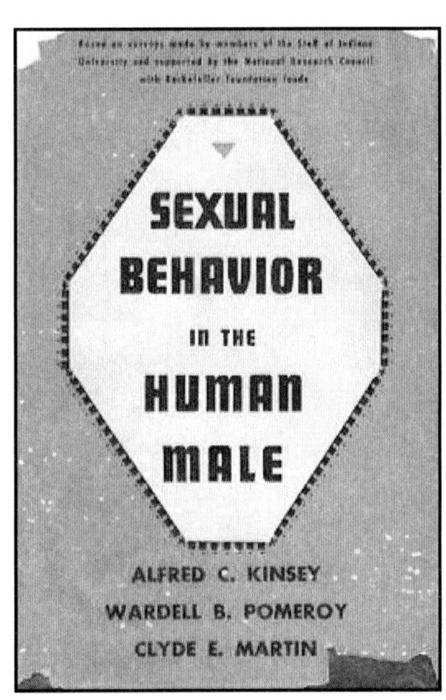


*Sexual Behavior in the Human Male*, published in 1948

(Image credit: Wikimedia Commons.)

A lot would change in the next twenty years. In this chapter, we'll look at the major events that brought us to the open declaration of the Sexual Revolution in the 1960s, and then on to the present moral wasteland in which we live today.

## CULTURAL LEADERS BECOME BRAZEN IN THE 1950S

> For this you know, that no fornicator, unclean person, nor covetous man, who is an idolater, has any inheritance in the kingdom of Christ and God. Let no one deceive you with empty words, for because of these things the wrath of God comes upon the sons of disobedience. Therefore do not be partakers with them. (Ephesians 5:5-7)

In **1950**, a graduate student at the University of Illinois named Hugh Hefner read Kinsey's book, and, inspired, wrote a college report urging changes in sex laws based on the Kinseyan view of human sexuality.

In the same year (**1950**), a communist dialectition named Harry Hay also read Kinsey's book. Likewise inspired to action, he formed the Mattachine Society, through which he argued that those 37% of American men who were supposedly homosexual were not committing sodomy, but were a "cultural minority" only seeking civil rights. He ended up being pretty successful using that argument, didn't he? (Years later, Harry Hay was a guest speaker for NAMBLA, the North American Man-Boy Love Association, where he encouraged attendees, "that the relationship with an older man is precisely what 13-, 14-, and 15-year-old [gay] kids need more than anything else in the world."[1])

Harry Hay founded the Mattachine Society.
(Image credit: Wikimedia Commons.)

[1] http://www.drjudithreisman.com/archives/2011/09/stop_sexualizin.html

Hugh Hefner, Kinsey's "pamphleteer".
(Image credit: Wikimedia Commons.)

Meanwhile, Kinsey's work was far from done. After the publication of *Sexual Behavior in the Human Male*, Kinsey began working on a follow-up volume; and in **1953**, *Sexual Behavior in the Human Female* was published. Kinsey claimed that for women to engage in premarital sex was beneficial for them, that women who kept themselves pure could cause long-lasting problems in their marriages, and that women who had abortions enhanced their sex lives.

Just as in the *Male* volume, Kinsey's claim to have studied average American women was a complete falsehood. Much of his "married" female data, for example, came from prostitutes who had lived with a man for more than a year. Together, the two volumes came to be called the Kinsey Reports.

Neither was Hugh Hefner idle during this time. In **1953**, he founded *Playboy* magazine; the premier issue boldly proclaimed in the cover, "First Time in any magazine Full Color the famous Marilyn Monroe Nude." Hefner became known as Kinsey's "pamphleteer" to Joe College. The magazine persuaded men to abandon love and protection of women for sex and recreation. Men learned to abandon duty toward women for selfish use—and often, abuse—of them.

Beginning in **1954**, *Playboy* published cartoons, and later photos, of children as sex objects. Eventually sodomy in marriage was touted as better than eye to eye, lip to lip married sex.

In **1955**, the Kinsey Reports were used by state commissions and revision committees to change laws. For example, in Draft #4 of the Model Penal Code issued that year, in the Sex Offenses Section, there are 197 footnotes in which Kinsey is listed as the sole authority on "normal" human sexual behavior.

The Supreme Court jumped on board in **1957**. The production and distribution of pornography was illegal, both in the states and under federal law. In the case *Roth v. United States*, Kinsey's lawyer, Morris Ernst, used the American Law Institute's new obscenity definition to defend Samuel Roth, a bookseller convicted of selling pornography. While the Court upheld Roth's conviction, they codified into their ruling the ALI's revised definition of obscentiy, legalizing pornography in America.

## THE GATES ARE THROWN WIDE OPEN IN THE 1960s

> And it came to pass, as soon as [Moses] came nigh unto the camp, that he saw the calf, and the dancing: and Moses' anger waxed hot, and he cast the tables out of his hands, and brake them beneath the mount.
>
> And when Moses saw that the people were naked... he said unto them, "Thus saith the Lord God of Israel, 'Put every man his sword by his side, and go in and out from gate to gate throughout the camp, and slay every man his brother, ... companion, and ... neighbour.'" (Exodus 32:19, 25, 27, KJV)

In **1960**, the U.S. Supreme Court again cited the ALI's definition of obscenity, and what was formerly illegal pornography is now called "soft pornography".

In **1961**, Illinois, home to Hefner and the *Playboy* headquarters, became the first state to legalize sodomy.

That same year (**1961**), the National Council of Churches (remember them?) held a conference in Green Lake, Wisconsin. The director of Planned Parenthood, Dr. Mary Calderone was scheduled to speak on family planning, encouraging church leaders to promote birth control, which was still illegal at that time. However, when she realized that the leaders were already on board with birth control, she shifted her topic to convincing church leaders to promote sex education to their church members.

Up through the 1920s, the protestant denominations in America had held to the historic Christian position against the use of contraception in marriage. The Lutheran Church-Missouri Synod, for example, called Margaret Sanger a "she devil" in 1921 for her promotion of birth control. But by **1963**, the protestants—even the conservative denominations—were on board with the limitation of family size, based on Alfred Kinsey's and Margaret Sanger's works. In 1964, for example, the same conservative denomination that had denounced birth control so forcefully before, the Lutheran Church-Missouri Synod, made an official announcement permitting its use. Many denominations did not record the change of position in official church documents, but it can be seen in the change in teachings, as well as the record of birth rates among clergy and church membership. (Note: Prior to 1965, it was still actually illegal for married couples to use contraception in America.)

Kinsey believed there was a need for sexual education for children, but that only "sexuality experts" who had been trained properly could do it. In **1964**, the Kinsey institute launched an initiative called the Sexuality Information and Education Council of the United States, or SIECUS. We'll be hearing a lot more about them throughout the book, so go ahead and learn that name now. SIECUS was designed to be a training program to create a new class of experts—sex experts, who could give children proper sex education. SIECUS became the educational arm for the Institute, and began putting sex education into all schools.

Meanwhile, not to be outdone by Indiana University and the Kinsey Institute, in **1964** New York University became the first college to offer a degree in Human Sexuality.

In **1965**, the Supreme Court decided to legalize the use of birth control use for married couples in its landmark *Griswold v. Connecticut* decision.

*Playboy* began funding SIECUS for the first time in **1967**. You might ask yourself, *Did* Playboy *stand to gain financially from their investment in SIECUS?*

Jefferson Airplane performing in June, 1967.
(Image credit: Wikimedia Commons.)

In **1967**, young people inspired by messages of "free love", drug use, and communal living came from across the country to gather in San Francisco. The media triumphantly declared that there had been a Sexual Revolution in what was dubbed the "Summer of Love". In truth, only a small minority of young people ever joined the hippy movement. And for the ones who had come to San Francisco in seach of Utopia, within months, they realized that "free love" often meant rape, drug use often led to drug addiction, and communism often meant your comrades stole from you when you weren't looking... and most of them made their way right back home to college or work. But the media told a story of Sexual Revolution.

And to crown a really spectacular decade for the family, in **1969**, the Presidential Commission on Obscenity & Pornography, counseled by the Kinsey Institute, ruled that pornography was entirely harmless.

## THE AFTERMATH: MORAL DECLINE

> "Beware of false prophets, who come to you in sheep's clothing, but inwardly they are ravenous wolves. You will know them by their fruits. Do men gather grapes from thornbushes or figs from thistles? Even so, every good tree bears good fruit, but a bad tree bears bad fruit." (Matthew 7:15–17)

The story that a Sexual Revolution occurred in 1967 may have largely been a construct of the media, but the changes in society and the church over the five decades since the Progressive Era had been real enough. There was a complacency in the culture; we'd defeated Hitler; we had the A-bomb; we went to the moon, for goodness' sake. American Christians weren't looking for another fight, and sadly they were blindsided and deceived by this one.

The New Testament warns the church again and again to be on our guard against being deceived—whether by someone inside or outside of the church. But those generations of Christians did not search the scriptures diligently to see whether or not these new ideas were so.

> [The Bereans] were more fair-minded than those in Thessalonica, in that they received the word with all readiness, and searched the Scriptures daily to find out whether these things were so.[2]

There was a revolution underway, but rather than fight for God's standard of modesty, purity, chastity, and self-control, the church compromised with the revolutionaries. And things began moving fast.

In academia, the Sexual Attitude Restructuring technique (SAR) was introduced in **1971** to restructure sexual attitudes away from the absolute standard of right and wrong, based on the Bible and borne out by honest research and experience, to Kinsey's fraudulent "standard" based on a depraved mind, supported by dishonest research, and disproven by experience. You'll hear more about SAR when we tell the tale of sex education in the next chapter.

Seven years after the Supreme Court "stuck down" all of the Christian laws against birth control use for married couples, in **1972**, the Supreme Court made birth control use legal for unmarried couples, too.[3]

The following year, in **1973**, the Supreme Court ruled that baby killing was legal in the United States with their *Roe v. Wade* decision.

Henry Blackmun authored the majority opinion in *Roe v. Wade*. (Image credit: Wikimedia Commons.)

In their decision, the Supreme Court cited the ALI, who relied on Kinsey's abortion data, as well as the testimony of Planned Parenthood's medical director, Mary Calderone, that "90 to 95 percent of premarital pregnancies are aborted."[4]

Every state government immediately ceased enforcement of their duly-enacted laws against baby killing.

> "And they built the high places of Baal which are in the Valley of the Son of

[2] Acts 17:11.

[3] *Eisenstadt v. Baird* (1972).

[4] http://www.drjudithreisman.com/archives/2005/08/sordid_science_2.html

> Hinnom, to cause their sons and their daughters to pass through the fire to Molech, which I did not command them, nor did it come into My mind that they should do this abomination, to cause Judah to sin." (Jeremiah 32:35)

You remember John Dewey, right? The father of modern American public schools? Committed humanist and socialist? Well, the public school system was faithfully carrying his vision forward. In **1973**, the president of the National Education Association (NEA) wrote,

> Dramatic changes in the way we will raise our children in the year 2000 are indicated, particularly in terms of schooling... We will need to recognize that the so-called 'basic skills,' which currently represent nearly the total effort in elementary schools, will be taught in one-quarter of the present school-day... When this happens... and it's near... the teacher can rise to his true calling. More than a dispenser of information, the teacher will be a conveyor of values, a philosopher... We will be agents of change.[5]

The NEA believes teachers should be "agents of change".

And of course you remember Sigmund Freud and the creation of psychiatry—how there were no sins anymore, just disorders? Right, well, the funny thing about that is that when something is labelled a *disorder* on the basis on some men's opinion, it's just as easy to *unlabel* it a disorder on the basis of some men's opinion. Which is exactly what they did with sodomy in 1974. When we were a Christian nation, basing our laws on God's laws, sodomy was considered sin, and the only way around that was to reject the Bible. But the young field of psychiatry named sodomy or homosexual behavior a *disorder*, until 1974, when the American Psychiatric Association changed its policy and decreed that homosexuality

---

[5] Catherine Barrett, in the *Saturday Review* of Education (February 10, 1973), https://tdn.com/opinion/letters/letters-teach-or-indoctrinate/article_7bef4dca-05cd-5c1b-a62e-8b401d221057.html

is now a normal sexual variation. They cited Kinsey and the National Institute of Mental Health (NIMH) Task Force reports to explain their new "understanding".

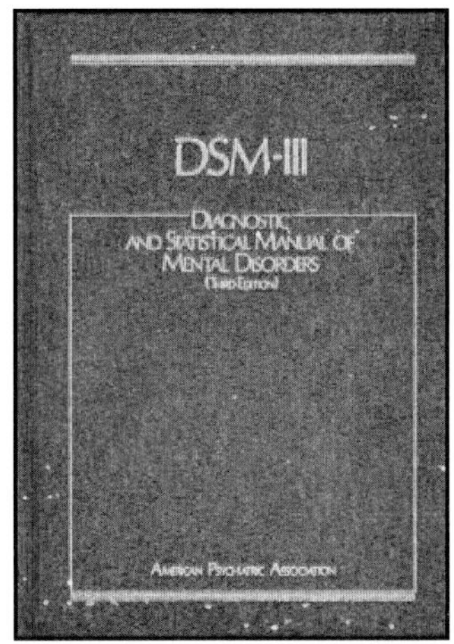


The American Psychiatric Association's *DSM-III*, begun in 1974.

(Image credits: Wikimedia Commons.)

The Supreme Court legalized birth control for minors (children under the age of 18) in **1977**.[6]

And in **1980**, Johns Hopkins University began performing the first "sex change" operations in the United States. Alfred Kinsey's bogus science influenced this decision, along with Dr. John Money who was an advocate for adult-child "sex" (rape) and transgender surgery.

Meanwhile, everyone with a fortune in America knows that the only way to keep your fortune tax-free is to put it all into charities that promote your vision for "helping" the world. And, boy, by this time, did Hugh Hefner have a fortune. In **1980**, *Playboy* funded People for the American Way and the American Library Association. Then, from **1981–1989**, *Playboy* funded Planned Parenthood. You can tell a lot about a charity by who funds it.

# MORAL DEVASTATION OVERTAKES SOCIETY, BUT THE CHURCH BEGINS TO AWAKEN

> But all things that are exposed are made manifest by the light... Therefore He says: "Awake, you who sleep, arise from the dead, and Christ will give you light." (Ephesians 5:13–14)

You're ready for some good news, aren't you? Consider this: You're reading this book. The lies are being exposed. God is waking us up!

---

[6] *Carey v. Population Control* (1977).

Dr. Judith Reisman is the most pivotal figure in the awakening of Christians from the deceitful and immoral ideas that so many of us had been taught on the authority of Kinsey's supposed "science". In **1990**, she published *Kinsey, Sex & Fraud*, which called out Kinsey's research as fraud for the first time. (You can read the book for free at drjudithreisman.com.)

Dr. Judith Reisman devoted her life to exposing the fraud Kinsey had perpetrated on the American people..

(Image credit: Wikimedia Commons.)

For forty-two years, Kinsey's claims had stood abolutely unchallenged, without even honest scientific scrutiny being applied to them. Finally, someone dared to do a little digging and see if the man behind the curtain was all the he claimed to be.



Dr. Judith Reisman courageously exposed Kiney's work as fraud.

(Image credit: Wikimedia Commons.)

In **1991**, she published *Soft Porn Plays Hardball*, in which she exposed the inner workings of Hugh Hefner and *Playboy*, including Hefner's connections to Kinsey. The unassailable authority of Kinsey's "science" was finally called into question.

In **1994**, Col. Ronald Ray, decorated former Marine and Deputy Assistant to the Secretary of Defense under the Reagan administration, together with his wife Eunice Ray, president of First Principles Press, established the Restoring Social Virtue and Purity to America (RSVP America) campaign. The goal of RSVP America was to exposing Kinsey's fraud science, and call legislators worldwide to repeal laws based on Kinsey's deceit. Dr. Judith Reisman joined the Rays to push this campaign across America; and national and state legislators, as well as top Christian leaders, were briefed that

From left: Linda Jeffrey, Eunice Ray, and Col. Ron D. Ray co-wrote the *RSVP Training Manual*, along with Dr. Judith Reisman.
(Image credit: Wikimedia Commons.)

the changes to American law over the past decades had not been based on science, but on Kinsey's fraud. They had a major impact in revealing the truth about Kinsey's "science".

Even while the good guys were beginning to push back, the bad guys continued moving forward with their agenda. We're getting into most of our lifetimes now, so most of us can remember the cultural push toward acceptance of sexual immorality in the 1990s and early 2000s, from *Murphy Brown* to *Will and Grace*. In **2001**, the family court handbook, *Principles of the Law of Family Dissolution,* was published, stating that,

> Some courts assume the open homosexuality of a parent is detrimental to the child's interests. This treatment reflects moral judgment, not a scientific one, and, even as a moral matter, is subject to considerable societal debate.[7] (Remember, it is Kinsey's "science" they are referring to!)

In the landmark **2003** Supreme Court decision, *Lawrence v. Texas*, Justice Anthony Kennedy cited Kinsey to strike down the last sodomy laws still standing in America. This decision opened the door for the "redefinition" of marriage. Because procreation was no longer established as a primary purpose for marriage—thanks to birth control, abortion, sodomy, and pornography—those who commit sodomy began to claim that that act was as rational a ground as any other to claim the status of legally "married" in the eyes of the law.

---

[7] *Principles of the Law of Family Dissolution*, 12.

In **2004**, the American Legislative Exchange Council (ALEC), the nation's largest voluntary membership organization of state legislators, with nearly 2,400 members, presented in their publication, *The State Factor*, a comprehensive analysis by Linda Jeffrey, PhD—a sister-in-arms who worked closely with Col. Ron Ray, Eunice Ray, and Judith Reisman—calling for the full restoration of legal protections for women and children in the states' criminal codes.[8] This was the first time a body of legislators not only acknowledged that Alfred Kinsey's research was fraudulent, but called for reform of our nation's laws.

AMERICAN LEGISLATIVE EXCHANGE COUNCIL

The State Factor

*Jeffersonian Principles in Action*

***Restoring Legal Protections for Women And Children: A Historical Analysis of The States Criminal Codes***

In 2004, ALEC published Linda Jeffrey's analysis exposing the changes to American law that had occurred in the name of Kinsey's fraud science.

(Image credit: Wikimedia Commons.)

In **2015**, the Supreme Court of the United States decreed in *Obergefell v. Hodges* that all of the duly-enacted state laws affirming the biblical definition of marriage were "unconstitutional", and that every state must recognize "marriages" between men and other men, or women with other women, in all of the same ways that the states recognize actual marriage. As with these other lawless decisions, the state governors and president immediately began enforcement of this opinion as if it had been law duly enacted by the legislature.

Blessed is the man
Who walks not in the counsel of the ungodly,...
But his delight is in the law of the Lord,
And in His law he meditates day and night.
...whatever he does shall prosper.

The ungodly are not so,
But are like the chaff which the wind drives away.
Therefore the ungodly shall not stand in the judgment,

[8] Dr. Linda Jeffrey, "Restoring Legal Protections for Women and Children: A Historical Analysis of the States' Criminal Code," *The State Factor* (April, 2004). You can read it for free at matthew18.org.

Nor sinners in the congregation of the righteous.
...The way of the ungodly shall perish. (Psalm 1)

## KINSEY AND THE CHURCH

Husbands, love your wives, just as Christ also loved the church and gave Himself for her, that He might sanctify and cleanse her with the washing of water by the word, that He might present her to Himself a glorious church, not having spot or wrinkle or any such thing, but that she should be holy and without blemish. (Ephesians 5:25–27)

This story is ultimately about the *church*, and how the Sexual Revolution impacted Christian churches.

There's no easy way to say this: The church has embraced Kinsey. Yes, conservative denominations rejected things that contradicted major laws of God, such as fornication, adultery, divorce, and homosexuality... but they accepted the underlying premise that Kinsey had made discoveries about human sexuality that were helpful, true, and needed to be accepted.

Before Kinsey, the church taught that the marital act and procreation were inextricably linked. After Kinsey, the church taught that the marital act should be separated from the bearing of children. Before Kinsey, the church taught that sodomy (even in marriage) was against God's order. After Kinsey, Christian books taught Christians that their marriages would be more fulfilling if they brought such practices into the marriage bed.

Christian books, seminar speakers, and pastors unknowingly teach Kinsey's fraudulent ideas.

Kinsey taught that the primary aim of sexual intercourse was orgasm. Before, the church had taught that the marital act was a blessing from God to reflect the joys and intimacy of the future union of the Christ and his Bride, as well as the means God institutued to carry out the life process.

Before Kinsey, again, the church taught the biblical view that the marital act was a gift from God, unlike other gifts in some ways, but certainly like other gifts in many ways! After Kinsey, the church taught (again) that the marital act is all about orgasm, and that orgasm is a *need*. For health, for satisfaction, for fulfillment.

The church as a whole swallowed all of these ideas from Kinsey as "science" without asking a single critical question.

> But fornication and all uncleanness or covetousness, let it not even be named among you, as is fitting for saints; neither filthiness, nor foolish talking, nor coarse jesting, which are not fitting, but rather giving of thanks. (Ephesians 5:3–4)

Chapter 4

# SEX EDUCATION: HISTORY

> But every man is tempted, when he is drawn away of his own lust, and enticed. Then, when lust hath conceived it bringeth forth sin: and sin, when it is finished, bringeth forth death. (James 1:14–15, KJV)

Sixty years ago, sex education was considered "molesting a minor with immoral intent" in American law.

For virtually all of us, the Sexual Revolution is very real and personal because we were indoctrinated into it from childhood. Americans born before 1948 may have been exposed to the literature and movies coming out of New York and Hollywood, but the sexual "liberation" they saw happening around them was largely... something happening to other people.

But Americans born after 1948 were "trained" in their science or health classes to believe Kinsey's doctrines. They were sexualized from their youth.

*We* were sexualized from our youth.

You now know the overarching story of the Sexual Revolution; here is the tale of how sex education became normalized for children.

# A HERO IN THIS FIGHT

> Blessed be the Lord my Rock, who trains my hands for war, and my fingers for battle... Rescue me and deliver me from the hand of foreigners, whose mouth speaks lying words, and whose right hand is a right hand of falsehood—that our sons may be as plants grown up in their youth; that our daughters may be as pillars, sculptured in palace style... Happy are the people who are in such a state; happy are the people whose God is the Lord! (Psalm 144:1, 11-12, 15)

You remember that during the late 1800s, a subculture of moral depravity was growing in Germany. In cities like New York, the same trends were underway... but something different happened in America. Actually, one man happened.

Anthony Comstock led a crusade against pornography, abortion, prostitution, and other forms of vice.
(Image credit: Wikimedia Commons.)

Anthony Comstock was born in Connecticut in 1844, where Puritan blood still flowed in the cultural veins; this was the state of Noah Webster, who died a mere nine months before Comstock's birth. His parents raised him in the faith, and he embraced our Lord and Savior Jesus Christ from his youth. Comstock fought in the Civil War, and shortly after the war's end, came to New York City, where he was horrified to witness a thriving sex trafficking industry openly promoted all over the city. Women and children were kept in sex slavery, brazen advertisements for this prostitution were to be found all over the city, obscene pornographic materials were freely distributed. It was unsafe for women or children to walk the streets alone. It was unsafe for anyone's moral character to walk the streets alone.[1]

---

[1] Judith Reisman, *Sexual Sabotage*, http://www.drjudithreisman.com/archives/2010/12/sexual_sabotage_1.html.

His inspiring story is too much to tell here, but suffice it to say that he devoted his life to crusading against the vice and licentiousness that was overtaking New York City and the rest of our country. It all began when a colleague was stricken by a venereal disease. The original cause of this coworker's fall into vice had been obscene materials—pornography, so Comstock marched over to the guilty printer's shop, took some of the materials as evidence to the police, and saw that operation shut down. A few like successes followed, and Comstock had found his life's calling.

By the time of his death in 1915, Comstock Laws, as they came to be called, had been passed across the nation, prohibiting the sale and distribution of obscenity, banning prostitution, and outlawing abortion. These were the laws that protected women and children, that the ALI's Model Penal Code specifically targeted for removal.

He was vilified in the press at the time, and still is in the writings of secular historians today, but because of his tireless efforts, New York (and other American cities) became safe places again for women and children.

Even so, we can never completely eradicate the devil's works, and there were plenty of pornographers and madams who managed to bribe judges to drop charges against them. The newspapers, suffragettes, and all of the other progressives never stopped mocking and fighting Comstock; and there were dedicated progressives and libertines prepared to fight to retake the ground they'd lost.

## THE EARLIEST CALLS FOR SEX EDUCATION

> "But whoever causes one of these little ones who believe in Me to sin, it would be better for him if a millstone were hung around his neck, and he were drowned in the depth of the sea." (Matthew 18:6)

The first open calls for sex education for America's youth began toward the end of Comstock's life.

In **1905**, a New York dermatologist named Dr. Prince Morrow was the first voice to sound this cry. He was concerned about the sexually transmitted disease rates in the city, and rejected Comstock's method of fighting the root cause—sin and vice. (The STD rates of Morrow's day were miniscule compared to today's rates, but they were disturbing at the time.) Like a good humanist, he founded the American Society for Sanitary and Moral Prophylaxis—a program that would fix our "societal ills". He argued that the answer to the STD epidemic was sex education for youth. He encouraged medical doctors to "educate" youth, because doctors had better scientific understanding about anatomy than parents had. Social hygienists began to substitute medical intervention for moral persuasion in the quest to prevent unwed pregnancy, venereal disease, and other "diseases of the social order".

National Education Association General Meeting, July 3, 1916.
(Image credit: Wikimedia Commons.)

Only seven years later—and while Anthony Comstock was still in the fight—in **1912**, the National Education Association realized that sex education was clearly something that needed to be in the basic school curriculum. They endorsed the American Society for Sanitary and Moral Prophylaxis, and began pushing for the training of school teachers in sex education and sex hygiene, to bring sex education into *schools*. Can you even imagine who would think that way? Best case scenario, they're thinking to themselves, *Parents aren't telling children all about marital intimacy and fidelity, or at least they don't know how to do it right; and these doctors who are telling youth all of the details in the privacy of the doctor's office, using their medical expertise to get it right, are on the right track.*

*But what we really need is to tell the kids all of the details in a classroom, with all of the other kids in there together.* There is no possible innocent explanation for this.

In **1921**, Margaret Sanger founded the American Birth Control League, which pushed for sex education in the schools. Remember, this wasn't a little effort that fizzled out... The American Birth Control League is called Planned Parenthood today, and Sanger herself lived until 1966, working diligently for her goals all the way to the end. She saw birth control made legal and sex education put in the schools. In your mind, don't just think of 1921, but think, *1921–present*.

## ONLY SIXTEEN YEARS

> I have seen the wicked in great power, and spreading himself like a native green tree. Yet he passed away, and behold, he was no more; indeed I sought him, but he could not be found. (Psalm 37:35-36)

You can see that, even though efforts were underway from the dawn of the twentieth century in America to sexualize children, not a whole lot of progress was made. But after the publication of Kinsey's book, it will take your breath away how quickly the devil won that crucial victory—indoctrination of our future generations. You will think the wicked men and women in this tale are in great power, spreading themselves like a native green tree. The story is sad, yes. And you need to know it, to know where we have come from and what you are up against as you endeavor to raise up your children in biblical purity. But if you find yourself growing discouraged, remember that these wicked men, and their wicked works, will pass away. One day, people will look for them, and not even remember so much as their names.

You already know that Kinsey's *Male* volume, in which he purported to demonstrate that "children are sexual from birth," was published in **1948**.

With this new "understanding", it was clear that all of the poor children were clearly suffering because of all the sexual "needs" they had which no one was equipping them to understand and fulfill. Sex education was clearly necessary, so that children could be educated in their "sexuality".

Prior to 1950, children were looked upon as morally innocent. God's life process was communicated to them through the example of the flower, the birds, and the bees. The little son or daughter was shown a flower, and shown about how the flower has a male part and a female part; and the child was told about how when a bee or a bird comes to drink the nectar from a flower, it can transfer the pollen from the male part over to the female part where the ovule is, where the two necessary parts of the seed unite and become a new seed—a new life.

But after 1950, there was a shift; parents and educators were told that children needed to be educated on anatomical names for their (and their classmates') private parts and given graphic descriptions of sex acts. (You might note that educators do not stress the importance of children calling their arms, or their legs, or their tummies, ears, fingers, or anything else by their "correct anatomical names", yet we are told that it is of the utmost importance that children call their private parts by their correct anatomical names.)

In **1950**, the Group for the Advancement of Psychiatry (GAP) recommended that children make sexual decisions at age seven. They suggested that "training" such as sex education was necessary to prepare them for sexual activity:

> [P]ersons under the age of 7 are legally regarded as not responsible... It may be true that such persons cannot enter into contracts, but many are by endowment and training fully capable of part or exceptionally even full responsibility for sexual behavior.[2]

The Group for the Advancement of Psychiatry is still active today. They were part of the early efforts to pioneer a new field of psychology called "marriage counseling".

In **1953**, Planned Parenthood physician Dr. Lena Levine explained the goal of sex education:

---

[2] Linda Jeffrey, Ed.D, "Restoring Legal Protections for Women and Children: A Historical Analysis of the States' Criminal Codes," *The State Factor* (April 2004), 5.

> [We must] be ready as educators and parents to help young people obtain sex satisfaction before marriage... and we must be ready to provide young boys and girls with the best contraception measures available so they will have the necessary means to achieve sexual satisfaction without having to risk possible pregnancy.[3]

As you remember, in **1957**, the *Roth v. U.S.* decision by the Supreme Court opened the door to allow pornographic materials into the classroom for "educational purposes".

In **1959**, the public schools in the District of Columbia were the first to bring sexually explicit materials into the classroom to teach children about sex. While most states have laws against showing obscenity to children, in forty-four states and Washington, D.C. there are "obscenity exemptions", based on Kinsey's "findings", which allow obscenity to be shown to children in classrooms and libraries "for educational purposes".

Then, in three years, everything about education in America changed. In **1962**, the Supreme Court forbade prayer in the schools in their *Engel v. Vitale* decision. In **1963**, the Supreme Court forbade the reading of the Bible in public schools, in their *Abington v. Schempp* decision. And in **1964**, SIECUS (Sexuality Information and Education Council of the United States) was launched at the Kinsey Institute, and Kinsey's humanist-based sex education to children which highlights sexual pleasure and birth control, was soon taught in every school in America.

Earl Warren presided over the Supreme Court as Chief Justice from 1953–1969, in what came to be known as the Warren Court.
(Image credit: Wikimedia Commons.)

Sixteen years after the publication of Kinsey's book, God was completely removed from the education of American children, and sexuality was put in.

---

[3] Lena Levine, "Psychosocial Development." *Planned Parenthood News* (Summer 1953), 10.

# THE SIX MAJOR PLAYERS OF SIECUS

> Therefore behold, I will once again deal marvelously with this people, wondrously marvelous; and the wisdom of their wise men will perish, and the discernment of their discerning men will be concealed. (Isaiah 29:14)

SIECUS isn't a single person like Alfred Kinsey, but it was made up of people. Just as when you hear *Planned Parenthood*, you think of Margaret Sanger and her bloodthirst for "erradicating" people she thought "less" than herself (or at least I hope you're starting to...), when you think of SIECUS, you need to think of the real people who wrote its materials, lobbied for its policies, and designed the program to create an army of "sex educators". There were six major founders of SIECUS who began this work in 1964; each represented a particular field of expertise which he was charged with influencing.

As you read about these men and women, try to think back to what you "understood" about sex ed before you started Knowing Your History. What kind of people did you think wrote sex education materials? What did you think their motivations were?

First, in the field of Medicine, we have **Dr. Mary Calderone**. Remember her, from *Roe v. Wade*? Her testimony was cited by Henry Blackmun in the court's decision to ban just punishments for murdering children in the womb. She was the first Medical Director for Planned Parenthood, serving in that position for eleven years, beginning in 1953. In 1964, she won a hard-fought victory when she convinced the American Medical Association to overturn its policy against giving birth control information to patients. Or, in

Dr. Mary Calderone was the Director of SIECUS, 1954–1982.
(Image credit: Wikimedia Commons.)

the words of a supporter, she convinced the AMA "to consider family planning as part of comprehensive health care."[4]

That's so hard for us to imagine; but just think—from the earliest settlement of our country until 1964, doctors thought it was wrong to tell patients about birth control methods. Four hundred fifty years... Americans didn't do *too* badly during that time.

As soon as she had secured that victory, Calderone left Planned Parenthood and founded SIECUS. This is such an interesting connection, because Planned Parenthood's incestuous tie with sex education is not merely philosophical; when children are given sex education, they grow up to become Planned Parenthood *customers*. Sex ed is a major advertising campaign for abortion and contraception providers.

SIECUS, as you know, had major funding from foundation grants. From the start, it had a large board of directors, and all six of the people we're learning about here were original founders. But Mary Calderone was the queen bee.

In 1974, Calderone was named "Humanist of the Year" by the American Humanist Association. She supported the works of author and humanist Rudolf Dreikurs who proposed reversing sexes and sex roles, "liberating" children from their families, and abolishing traditional families.

This is who designed sex ed.

Next, in the field of church ministry, meet **Rev. William Genné**, who devoted himself to the work of sex education in the church. Bet you didn't see that coming, did you?

Remember how these Marxists were savvy, and were intentional about infiltrating one of the most important organizations in America, the church? And remember that the sex ed movement is made up of communists? It's just strategy for them.

> For such are false apostles, deceitful workers, transforming themselves into apostles of Christ. And no wonder! For Satan himself transforms himself into an angel of light. Therefore it is no great thing if his ministers also transform themselves into ministers

[4] https://www.rochester.edu/newscenter/mary-calderone-your-sexuality-is-yourself-as-the-total-person-you-are-369602/

> of righteousness, whose end will be according to their works. (2 Corinthians 11:13–15)

Genné associated with at least three communist front groups, such as the "Committee for Peaceful Alternatives to the Atlantic Pact", etc. He rejected the idea of moral absolutes, and promoted situational ethics. He was the Director for the National Council of Churches' Commission on Marriage and Family Life and served on the board for *Sexology* magazine, a publication that was like a shockingly sick and twisted *Playboy*.

He and his wife traveled around giving talks in churches across the nation and internationally, frequently wrote for denominational publications, and coauthored several books including *The Ministry of Parents* (what "ministry" do you suppose an original founder of SIECUS and board member of *Sexology* told Christian parents they needed to fulfill?), and *Christians and the Crisis in Sex Morality* (pretty rich, coming from one of the men who caused the "crisis" in sex morality!). He and his wife were a team in this work.

William and Elizabeth Genné, promoted by a newspaper article encouraging the Scarsdale, NY community to attend their Marriage Enrichment series at Hitchcock Presbyterian Church, in 1976.
(Image credit: https://news.hrvh.org/.)

If you have gone to marriage seminars or conferences through a church or Christian organization, which taught about "sexual fulfillment", you need to know that SIECUS originally designed those. That's what William and Elizabeth Genné developed, and churches have been following their lead ever since. (Notice, by the way, that these conferences and seminars didn't originally advertize that they were going to talk about what husbands and wives ought to be doing in the marriage bed, and that the bedroom wasn't the whole topic, but once they got Christians there, the speakers surprised couples with talk about what they ought to be doing in bed.)

If you have read Christian books about marriage, which included tips about how husbands and wives should better "satisfy" each other in the marriage bed, or discussing the marital act as if the author is a doctor giving husbands and wives good medical-health advice, you need to know that SIECUS is the original author of that information. Again, William and Elizabeth Genné authored the books that first taught this to the church, and the church has been following their lead ever since.

When you were a youth, if you went through a "purity" program at church which emphasized how *wonderful* the marital act is, turning your mind to think and learn more about sexual intercourse, but then putting a Christian "band-aid" on all of that sexualization they were doing to you by saying, *But don't do it til you're married!...* You need to know that SIECUS is the author and creator of all of this sexualization that is done in the name of Christ in the church.

There are many well-meaning Christians today teaching this information, because they were taught it when they were children and they don't know any differently. But they are teaching Kinsey, straight up. The church has never done any of this before, in 2,000 years of Church history. You have William Genné, SIECUS founder and communist, to thank for skillfully convincing the church to get on the Kinsey bandwagon with the rest of the culture.

**Dr. Clark Vincent** represented the field of Behavioral Science. The Director of Behavioral Science at Bowman Gray School of Medicine at Wake Forest University, Vincent was on staff with *Sexology* magazine, believed in situational ethics, and served as editor for a textbook for medical students on human sexuality.

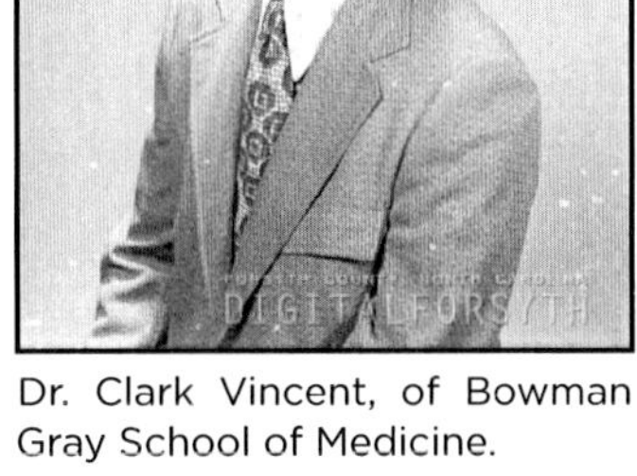

Dr. Clark Vincent, of Bowman Gray School of Medicine.
(Image credit: Digital Forsyth.)

In her telling book, *The SIECUS Circle*, Claire Chambers explained why a behavioral science expert was needed in the implementation of sex education:

> The ultimate goal is to establish scientific control over individuals and society. A primary vehicle used to achieve this goal is "sensitivity training"

> (SAR), a technique developed by humanists and strongly advocated by SIECUS.[5]

Advertisement for SAR in Tennesee, from 2019.

What, exactly, is Sexual Attitude Restructuring? Judith Reisman quotes a "very liberal" attendee to a 1982 SAR training who described his experience:

> The sensory overload culminated on Saturday night in a multi-media event... in the darkness... images of human beings—and sometimes even animals—engaging in every conceivable sexual act... Over a period of several hours... The subjects were nude... I felt myself becoming disoriented... Soon I realized that to avoid vertigo and nausea I would have to give up the attempt to discriminate and simply surrender to the experience... By the end... Nothing was shocking... But nothing was sacred either. But as I drove home, I began to get a slightly uneasy feeling. It was almost as if I had been conned... love had not been mentioned a single time during the entire weekend.[6]

These are the guys who created sex ed.

So this would be a great time to turn to the field of Education. **Wallace Fulton** helped to develop the "School Health Education System" in 1967. He was the first president of SIECUS. The School Health Education System included a program that employed SAR sensitivity training. It treated sex in a nihilistic manner, without any moral restraints. He used pornographic pictures to educate children and pitted the child against the parent.

Wallace Fulton, from the National Council on Family Relations archives.
(Image credit: NCFR.)

He was an elected member of the Board of Directors of the National Council on Family Relations (William Genné was heavily involved with them too, by the way), which worked to eliminate

---

[5] Claire Chambers, *The SIECUS Circle: A Humanist Revolution* (Belmont, MA: Western Islands, 1977), 22–23.

[6] http://www.drjudithreisman.com/archives/RSVP-optim.pdf.

spanking, encourage family structures other than the two-parent (father and mother) household, and offered talks at their conferences such as, for example at a conference focusing on family violence in 1970, "A New Look at Marriage", "Cultural Barriers to Family Limitation", "Sharing Session for Family Life Educators [sex educators] in Secondary Schools", "The Inexpressive Male: A Barrier to Healthy Male-Female Relationships", and "The Roots of Violence Develop within the Family".[7]

Harriet Pilpel was a liberal feminist and ACLU lawyer.

(Image credit: Wikimedia Commons.)

In the field of Law, **Harriet Pilpel**, a lawyer and past trustee to two humanist organizations, would guide the effort. Her resumé included work as vice-chairman for the ACLU, general counsel for Planned Parenthood, and work in practice with Kinsey's lawyer, Morris Ernst (who helped to draft the Model Penal Code using Kinsey's "science").

In 1950, a U.S. Customs agent, shocked at all of the "grossly obscene" materials constantly coming into the Kinsey Institute, began impounding it under the Comstock Act. Pilpel was one of the three lawyers who defended the Kinsey Institute. When the Supreme Court overturned the Comstock Act in the name of Kinsey's "research", Pilpel and her comrades finally won the "right" for the Kinsey Institute to receive obscene materials... for purposes of "research".

Finally, in the field of Psychology, allow me to introduce **Lester Kirkendall**. Kirkendall was a psychologist; he would become one of the most-cited "experts" in sex education.

He served on the Board of Penthouse Forum and was active in Planned Parenthood. He was a director of the American Humanist Association, a signer of Humanist Manifesto II, and 1983's Humanist of the Year.

Lester Kirkendall, pictured in the 20th anniversary issue *SIECUS Report*.

[7] https://history.ncfr.org/wp-content/uploads/2013/01/1970-conference-program.pdf

# Forums To Present Campus Sex Talk

Want to be a sexpert?

Forums may provide you with the opportunity on Monday when it presents Dr. Lester A. Kirkendall, professor of family life education at Oregon State University, who will speak on "Sex on the College Campus."

Dr. Kirkendall, noted psychologist, behavioral scientist, consultant and author, has achieved international recognition as an authority on family life, sex and marriage.

He will conduct an open informal discussion with students at 3:30 p.m. in room 204 of the Student Center. Following this he will present his keynote address at 7:30 p.m. in the Student Center ballroom.

He will reflect upon the issues with which he is concerned in his book, "Premarital Intercourse and Interpersonal Relationships."

Prior to this he will address Dr. Ronald C. Engle's 9 a.m. introductory sociology class.

**200 Articles**

Dr. Kirkendall has had eight full length books published and over 200 articles. His works have appeared in a wide assortment of publications, such as "School and Society," "Sexology," "Educational Digest" and "Playboy."

He has lectured at colleges and universities throughout the nation and in other countries.

His books include "Sex Adjustment of Young Men," "Understanding Sex," "Dating Days," "Sex Education as Human Relations," "Understanding The Other Sex," "Too Young to Marry?" and "Sex and Our Society."

He has also written an imposing sounding volume titled "A Reading and Study Guide for Students in Marriage and Family Relations."

Dr. Kirkendall, age 68, has been at Oregon State since 1948.

He received his Ph.D. from Columbia University in 1937 and once held a position with the U.S. Office of Education as a specialist in sex education.

**Adviser to Deans**

He is a founder of the Sex Education and Information Council of the U.S. and a director of the Association of Family Living in Chicago.

Because of his prominence in his field he often serves as adviser to deans, principals and other administrators. He deals with subjects which in other generations were not openly discussed.

Dr. Engle, who will join in the dialogue, says Dr. Kirkendall keeps in close touch with students and much of the material in his books is the result of talks with students.

His research is done in fields "a lot of people are hesitant to get into," said Dr. Engle.

He also appears to have the wholehearted support of the administration at his university, something which is apparently not easily acquired when dealing with this field.

On the front page of Texas Christian University's April 28, 1970 issue of the campus newspaper, across from a picture of pretty co-eds decorating for the school dance with an "old Southern garden" theme, students are encouraged to attend a talk given by Lester Kirkendall, visiting professor of "family life" from Oregon State.

(Image credit: repository.tcu.edu.)

Kirkendall was also a financial contributor to the "Temple of Understanding" in New York (TOU), who refer to themselves as the "spiritual United Nations". Margaret Sanger was also a member of the TOU, and they sponsored the Lucis Trust, whose publication is titled *Lucifer* magazine.

According to Judith Reisman, Kirkendall "believed that sex education was a prerequisite for public acceptance of population control—as well as for the modification of laws governing sex crimes, pornography and abortion."[8]

He wrote such books as *Premarital Intercourse and Interpersonal Relationships* and *Sex In the Childhood Years: Expert Guidance for Parents, Counselors, and Teachers.*

8 http://www.drjudithreisman.com/archives/Special_Report_-_Exposing_SIECUS.pdf

He was also a frequent contributor to good old *Sexology* magazine, writing articles like "Group Sex Orgies", "My Wife Knows I'm a Homosexual", and "Can Humans Breed with Animals?" He suggested a revision of *Sexology* for use in the public schools.[9]

As part of SIECUS's sex education materials for use in the schools, Kirkendall cowrote *Sex In the Adolescent Years: New Directions in Guiding and Teaching Youth*.

These are the people who created sex ed. They were never trying to educate kids so they wouldn't engage in premarital sex; they were devoted to taking innocent children and making them not only sexually active, but sexually deviant.

## WHAT HAPPENED NEXT

> And they said, "Come, let us build ourselves a city, and a tower whose top is in the heavens; let us make a name for ourselves, lest we be scattered abroad over the face of the whole earth." (Genesis 11:4)

In **1964**, UNESCO (United Nations Educational, Scientific, and Cultural Organization) sponsored an International Symposium on Health Education, Sex Education, and Education for Home and Family Living in West Germany. Julian Huxley—yep, the grandson of agnostic Thomas Huxley and brother of *Brave New World* author Aldous Huxley—was the first Director of UNESCO. In 1948, he had written about UNESCO's purpose:

> [E]ven though it is quite true that any radical eugenic policy (controlled human breeding) will be for many years politically and psychologically impossible, it will be important for UNESCO to see that the eugenic problem is examined with the greatest care, and that the public mind is informed of the issues at stake so that much that now is unthinkable may at least become thinkable.[10]

---

[9] http://www.fbbc.com/messages/hyles_sex_education.htm

[10] Claire Chambers, *The SIECUS Circle: A Humanist Revolution* (Belmont, MA: Western Islands, 1977), 5.

Did you read that? The purpose of UNESCO is eugenics. Remember that, the next time you hear CNN or Fox News tell you what UNESCO says, as if they are some sort of reputable authority.

But as for the topic at hand—the very year that SIECUS was born, Julian Huxley was already promoting sex ed at UNESCO. The influential players in this movement were Americans, and they would use the credibility and influence of the United States and her Christian heritage as vehicles to export their doctrines around the world. One of the conclusions from this symposium was that "sex education [should] begin at the primary school level." For every child in the entire world.

In **1966**, Ortho Pharmaceutical company, one of the largest manufacturers of the birth control pill, held a Symposium on Sex Education which was dominated by SIECUS officials. At the symposium, Arthur E. Gavett, M.D., stated:

> What shall be taught, has been sharply redefined by the current theological dialogue concerning ethics. The morality or immorality of any behavior, including sexual behavior has been put in the context of "situational ethics." In this approach moral behavior may differ from situation to situation. Behavior might be moral for one person and not another. Whether an act is moral or immoral is determined by "the law of love," that is the extent of which love and concern for others is a factor in relationships.[11]

Are you noticing that all of these foundations and the institutions spoke as if with one voice? One of them may have spoken first, but the newspapers, scientific organizations, educational establishments—all of which were funded by the same foundations—quickly chimed in to push the new ideas into acceptance.

In **1967**, the American Association of Sex Educators and Counselors (later renamed the American Association of Sex Educators, Counselors, and Therapists, or AASECT) was established by SIECUS leadership to ensure that all sex educators in the country were receiving the same SAR training and were *accredited* by them to teach sex to children. After the American Legislative Exchange Council (ALEC) was founded in 1973, they wrote about AASECT in their publication, *The State Factor*, saying:

---

[11] "Proceedings of a Symposium on Sex Education of the College Students," *Journal of the American College Health Association*, Vol. 15 (May 1967), 63.

> AASECT's job is to provide sex information to the sex educator, train him/her in the psychotherapy techniques necessary to communicate this knowledge to others, and restructure his/her sexual values so as to equip him/her to expand their students' tolerance and acceptance of variant sexual practices and lifestyles.[12]

When they told you at church or on your Christian radio program that it was important to tell your children all about sex, did they tell you that one of the goals of sex education is "to expand [your] students' tolerance and acceptance of variant sexual practices and lifestyles?"

In that same year, **1967**, the first Christian sex education series was published by the conservative Lutheran Church-Missouri Synod's Concordia Publishing House. The series was called the *Learning About Sex* series. Every conservative denomination in America used it for the first few decades it was out, until enough of the churches' youth who had been trained in sex ed grew up and became the new generation of leaders in those denominations, and they made their own materials, following the template of the *Learning About Sex* series.

*Wonderfully Made*, by Ruth Hummel; part of the original *Learning About Sex* series. Looks so sweet, doesn't it?

(Image credit: vintagekidsbooks.blogspot.com.)

Concordia lists the authorites whose expertise they relied upon to create this series for Christian children: Alan Guttmacher of Planned Parenthood; Lester Kirkendall, president of the American Humanist Association; and SIECUS. Kinsey's statistics are directly quoted in their book for parents.

America's youth were being sexualized and indoctrinated into sexual immorality in the public schools and the culture at large. There were

[12] Linda Jeffrey, Ed.D, "Restoring Legal Protections for Women and Children: A Historical Analysis of the States' Criminal Codes," *The State Factor* (April 2004), 5.

Christian parents who were alarmed at the new teachings, who either opted their children out of sex ed or even pulled their children out of the public schools entirely to send them to Christian schools. But what did these parents find in their church libraries to teach their children? And what did Christian school students learn in their classrooms? Kinsey's and SIECUS's doctrines, just the same:

- A significant portion of the population has natural homosexual tendencies and desires.
- Most men commit fornication before marriage (which is true now, but it wasn't then!).
- Sexual release is needed for health.
- Men hit their sexual "peak" in their teens (said the pedophile).
- If unmarried people are not taught about sexual intercourse as well as perverted sexual practices, they will become sexually frustrated and unhealthy.
- Physically, all forms of sexual release are healthy and equal.
- Husbands and wives should engage in sodomy together for the good of their marriage.
- Children are sexual from birth, and they need to be given information about sexual intercourse in childhood.

Now that you know names like Alfred Kinsey, Mary Calderone, Lester Kirkendall, SIECUS, and others, you can evaluate a Christian book that *claims* to teach the biblical perspective on marriage or purity, by looking at the sources the author refers to as his authority about human sexuality; you can see for yourself: *Is this author trusting God's Word about human "sexuality", or is he believing Alfred Kinsey's fraudulent claims of "scientific research"?*

Is a Christian sex ed material *really* Christian? Be very careful; the SIECUS- and Kinsey-based "Christian" sex ed materials all contain Bible verses, and a lot of correct Christian theology. And these days, a lot of the Christian authors on this topic actually mean well; they just have no idea how untrustworthy the information they've been taught to believe is. Be careful.

In **1969**, the National Education Association, American Medical Association, National Council of Churches, and American School Health Association all called for sexuality training for children.

In **1971**, the (Nixon) White House Conference on Youth endorsed universal sex education for elementary and secondary schools.

Then, from the **late 1970s** through the **1980s**, there was a (predicatble) epidemic of sexually transmitted diseases, particularly a new and deadly one called AIDS. This epidemic occurred in the homosexual and drug abuser communities, but it was used by all of the usual suspects as a supposed further rationale of the necessity of sex education in the schools, and the myth of "safe sex" (or condom use) was added to the children's curriculum.

Beginning in the **1990s** through the **present day**, homosexuality and bisexuality have been taught in the schools.

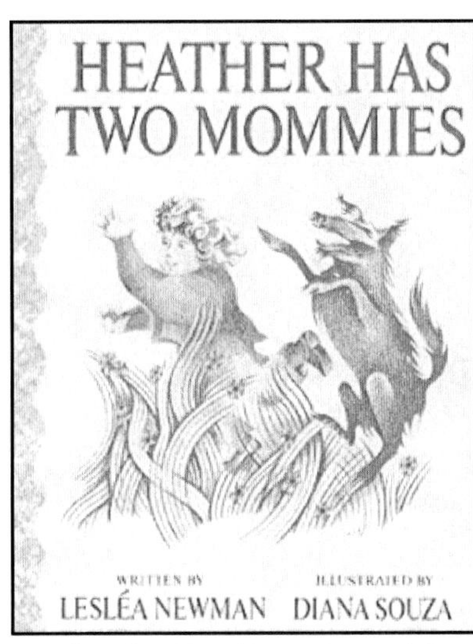


*Heather Has Two Mommies*, a picture book positively portraying lesbianism, has been promoted to children in schools and libraries across America.

(Image credit: Wikimedia Commons.)

And **now**, children are being taught about *when* to "consent" to sexual acts with other children and adults. Children continue to be exposed to obscenity to this very day.

Sex education was designed to titillate children and adults, not to educate in hygiene or prevent diseases. In sex education classes, children are taught to consider sexual pleasure outside of marriage, get an abortion if a conception occurs, and explore every type of sexual lifestyle (LGBTQ...).

This history should be disturbing to any parent.

Chapter 5

# Sex Education: Results

> But there were also false prophets among the people, even as there will be false teachers among you, who will secretly bring in destructive heresies, even denying the Lord who bought them, and bring on themselves swift destruction.
> (2 Peter 2:1)

Know Your History!

We were *indoctrinated* into the Sexual Revolution, and we needed some serious *deprogramming* so we could see clearly again, to be able to teach our children according to biblical principles. Now that you know the history of sex education and the Sexual Revolution, you understand the cause of the moral decline in America. But before we move on—to make sure we're not just making fuzzy claims about causes and effects like the sex educators do—we're going to briefly *quantify* the moral decline that has occurred since the introduction of sex education into Americans' lives. Let's take a look at the results.

Dr. Miriam Grossman, a child and adolescent psychiatrist, tells of the origins of sex ed in *You're Teaching My Child What?* She opens the book with a dire warning:

> Parents, if you believe that the goals of sexuality education are to prevent pregnancy and disease, you are being hoodwinked... Given that sex education has been in existence for over 60 years, we

> have plenty of data which validates the results.[1]

What results? For a woman of my generation, the moral decline in America is obvious. My generation has witnessed it happening all around us. But for my younger readers, let me give you a picture of what happened in America in only two or three decades. In that short period of time, our country was completely transformed.

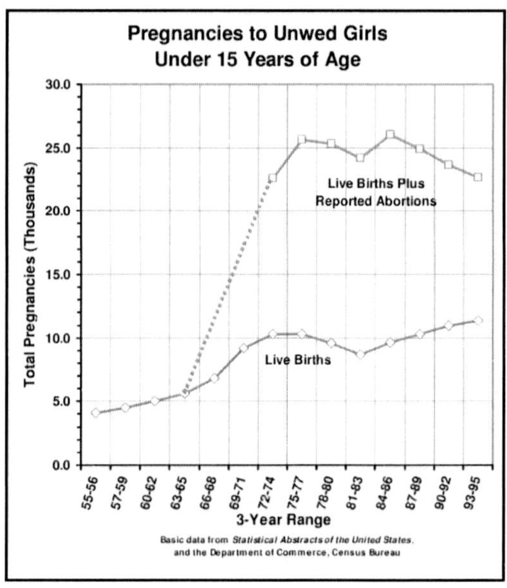


Moral Decline after the institution of sex education in America: Above, Pregnancy Rates under Age 15, 1955–1995. Below, Unwed Birth Rates for Ages 15–19, 1951–1996.

I think of this verse from Jeremiah:

> Thus says the Lord: "Stand in the ways and see, and ask for the old paths, where the good way is, and walk in it; then you will find rest for your souls.[2]

What was our country like, before sex education? What were the "old paths" like?

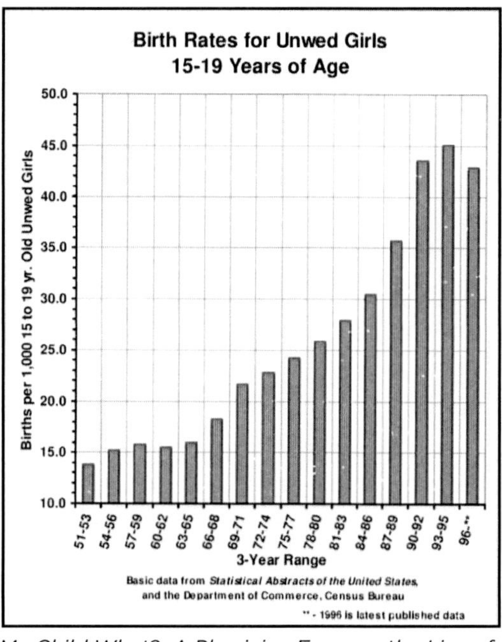


When I was growing up, most people considered themselves to be Christians, and more or less acted like it. Theft was rare. Murder was rare and shocking. Rape, homosexuality, and sexually transmitted

[1] Miriam Grossman, M.D., *You're Teaching My Child What?: A Physician Exposes the Lies of Sex Ed and How They Harm Your Child* (Washington D.C.: Regency Publishing, Inc., 2009), 7.

[2] Jeremiah 6:16

diseases were unthinkable in the average American's life. Unwed pregnancy and abortion were very rare. People could read, write, do math in their heads, and even knew America's history.

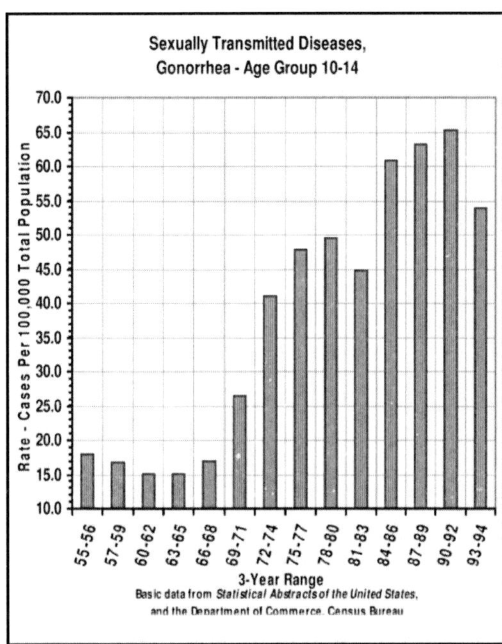


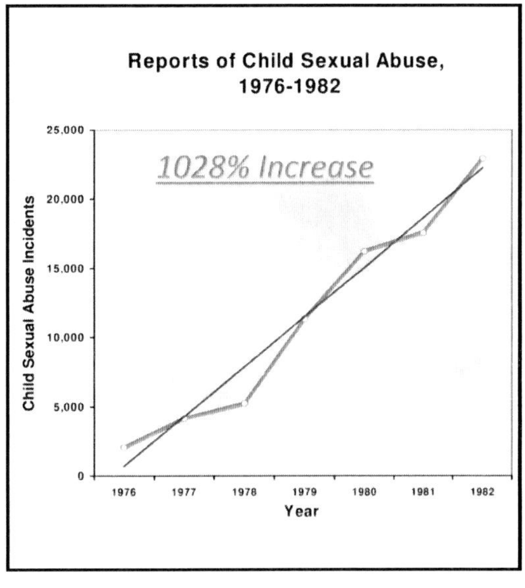


Moral Decline after the institution of sex education in America: Above, STD Rates Ages 10–14, 1955–1994. Below, Child Sexual Abuse, 1976–1982.

People treated each other with kindness and respect. Men showed deference to women, and fulfilled their duty toward women and children to protect them, even at the cost of their own lives. I grew up hearing stories of the sinking of the Titanic, where there were not enough lifeboats, and almost all of the survivors were woman and children, as the men cried, "Women and children first!" My parents' generation had demonstrated the same for us, when millions of America's young men stood in long lines to sign up to fight and die in World War II, that their women and children back home might be kept safe from the ruthless Japanese and German conquerors.

Whether a person was a Christian or not, the imaginary suffering of the sinful pervert like Kinsey or Sanger who felt that he or she "suffered" from not being able to live out their sexually deviant practices openly is nothing compared to the heartache and suffering millions of Americans have experienced since the Sexual Revolution—whether it be from sexually transmitted disease, abortion, or the rise in infertility; the explosion of rape, child sexual abuse, and gender confusion (which is another form of child sexual abuse); or skyrocketing depression, suicide, divorce, and fatherless homes. And of course the greatest suffering is the suffering of the person who dies apart from Christ, and spends eternity in Hell: The loss of faithful Christian teaching, through the weakening of the cultural influence of the Church in America, has far graver consequences than the ones we can display in our charts.

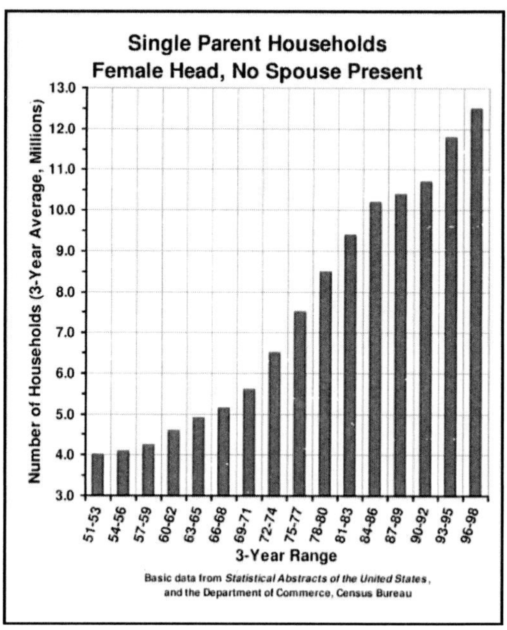

Moral Decline after the institution of sex education in America: Fatherless Homes, 1951–1998.

The charts in this chapter lay out in stark numbers the dramatic changes that my generation witnessed almost overnight, after we began sexualizing American children through sex education. And the numbers only got worse from there. In her book, *Epidemic: How Teen Sex Is Killing Our Kids*, pediatrician Meg Meeker puts together a current snapshot of the state of health for our youth. Our modern method of sex education is killing our children:

- Currently, the CDC reports that we have the highest recorded rates of sexually transmitted diseases since we began keeping records on them.[3]
- 1 out of every 5 adolescents is living with an STD.
- In 1960, a shot of penicillin could kill the two known STDs—syphilis and gonorrhea; but today there aren't simple cures, or there are no cures at all.
- The CDC considers the STD epidemic a multiple epidemic of at least 25 separate diseases (over fifty, if you count variant strains of viruses).

[3] https://www.cdc.gov/nchhstp/newsroom/docs/factsheets/std-trends-508.pdf

- Human Papilloma Virus (HPV), just one STD, is directly responsible for 99.7% of cervical cancer cases, at nearly 5,000 deaths in America each year.
- 80% of STD-infected kids are unaware that they have an STD.
- Half of all new HIV infections are in our youth (male and female).
- Condoms do not offer protection for most STDs.[4]

Continually, there are new words we're told we must use, to cover up the unpleasant results of our new morality. For example, STDs—sexually transmitted diseases—have now been renamed sexually transmitted *infections* (STIs). Contracting a disease has a much worse stigma than getting an infection; after all, doesn't everyone get an infection once in a while?

> Beloved, do not believe every spirit, but test the spirits, whether they are of God; because many false prophets have gone out into the world. (1 John 4:1)

It is interesting to note that, as our society's sexual agenda moved forward—whether in entertainment or in educational settings, the benefits of monogamy were seldom, if ever, mentioned. Meanwhile, sex outside of the confines of marriage and the "thrill" associated with this practice was (and is) exalted. The risks of sexual promiscuity—such as pregnancy and long-term intimacy issues—are never mentioned; the good-looking main character of the happy television show never gets infected with a sexually transmitted disease.

Getting to the root of the problem of sex education has been no easy task. Most people are unwilling to take an honest look at where things stand, but the blatant neglect of the data staring us in the face has been devastating for our young people.

Most of us can well remember sitting in our first sex education presentation. Perhaps you're reading this book in the hope that you will not have to repeat that experience with your child—this time with *you* being the one doing the teaching, and your precious child being the one going through the experience you remember not-so-fondly!

---

[4] Meg Meeker, M.D., *Epidemic: How Teen Sex is Killing Our Kids* (Washington, D.C.: LifeLine Press, 2002), 13.

## 10 Tips on How NOT to Talk to Your Kids about Sex

For too long we have been following the "experts'" advice on how to communicate the truth to our children about the life process, their bodies, and their future as husbands or wives. It is time for a change; it is time for parents to revolt and return to the old paths.

Let's find out how NOT to talk to your kids about sex.

> Test all things, hold fast what is good. Abstain from every form of evil. Now may the God of peace Himself sanctify you completely; and may your whole spirit, soul, and body be preserved blameless at the coming of our Lord Jesus Christ. He who calls you is faithful, who also will do it. Brethren, pray for us. (1 Thessalonians 5:21–25)

# Part II:

# 10 Tips!

Chapter 1

# Tip 1: More Is Caught Than Is Taught

If the foundations be destroyed, what can the righteous do? (Psalm 11:3 KJV)

When I wanted to learn how to pray for my husband, I purchased Stormie Omartian's book, *The Power of a Praying Wife*. I could not wait to learn how to better help and encourage my husband. However, I was disappointed to find that the first chapter—the longest chapter in the book—was about "His Wife." Stormie taught a great deal about being a godly wife first, before turning to how she learned to pray for her husband. She challenged me, and I began to ponder: *What is missing in my relationship with God, and where is my focus? Is it on his heart or on mine? Am I ignoring my sins and only concentrating on fixing my husband?* That first chapter was very humbling to read, but it was the most impactful part of the book. (I think every wife should read it.)

The same is true for parents. Before we can teach our children about purity, we have to repent of past failures and make sure that we are modeling purity to our kids. This will require an honest inquiry into our own activities and may even require a time of repentance and changes in behavior.

In the book, *The Battle Plan for Prayer*, Stephen and Alex Kendrick share something to consider:

> Victory necessitates repentance. Repentance helps you stand strong against temptation. But there's a difference between being tempted by something and being tormented by something. Everyone is tempted. Jesus was. You will be. It's not a sin to be tempted. But if the enemy is consistently tormenting you with something, there's a good chance unconfessed sin from your past has given him a foothold (a network of lies) in your heart (2 Corinthians 10:3–5).[1] Though the truth will set us free, lies can keep us in bondage.[2]

Many of us comprise the first or second generation exposed to wide-scale "sex education", and we live with the tragic consequences. It's easy to see the degrading, even shocking sexual sin all around us; but the difficult question to answer is, *How many of* us *are carrying around sexual sins that have never been repented of?*

The children of this generation are under more spiritual attack than any previous generation, and the techniques for leading little ones to sexual sin has been perfected by the enemies of Christ. You and I had fornication and abortion sold to us; our children face much more. They need healthy parents to help equip them to withstand those attacks.

When I speak about purity across the country, I hear the same response again and again: *I wish I had heard this purity message when I was young, because my life would have turned out differently!*

Don't allow past sins to keep you silent in regard to encouraging a pure life for your children. If you do, Satan has accomplished a major victory in the battle for your family. He wants to carry forward any legacy of sexual immorality that began in your family and pass it down to the next generation—and he has momentum on his side. You must take affirmative action to alter this momentum.

---

[1] For though we walk in the flesh, we do not war according to the flesh. For the weapons of our warfare are not carnal but mighty in God for pulling down strongholds, casting down arguments and every high thing that exalts itself against the knowledge of God, bringing every thought into captivity to the obedience of Christ.... (2 Corinthians 10:3-5)

[2] Stephen and Alex Kendrick, *The Battle Plan for Prayer* (Nashville, TN: B & H Publishing, 2015), 174–175.

The time is now for us to return to God's Word and do what He asks us to do while on this earth. In God's providence, you are learning the truth about biblical purity now; it wasn't earlier, but it is *now*, and you can trust His perfect plan for you on the timing of these things. When He convicts us of an area of sin in our lives, He is calling us to obey Him by putting it away from us. We need to look to our Lord as a loving parent who set up boundaries for us so that we will not be hurt. Those who promoted the Sexual Revolution tried to convince us that abstaining from fornication was wrong and even harmful. God knew otherwise. Just as parents know that allowing our children to run in the street could get them killed, God knew what would happen to us if we turned from His Word.

He knew if we were in multiple sexual relationships, it would be hard to remain married to only one person. He knew the pain we would experience if we went through a divorce. Actually, He is so much more than simply a Father to us; He is also our Creator, the one who designed our bodies down to every last molecule. He gave us bonding hormones which are triggered during the procreative act to seal the bond between a husband and wife—oxytocin for women and vasopressin in men.

God gave us the path that we should follow:

> For this is the will God, your sanctification[3]: that you should abstain from sexual immorality; that each of you should know how to possess his own vessel [your own body] in sanctification and honor, not in passion of lust, like the Gentiles who do not know God; that no one should take advantage of and defraud his brother in this matter, because the Lord is the avenger of all such, as we also forewarned you and testified. God did not call us to uncleanness, but in holiness. Therefore, he who rejects this does not reject man, but God, who has also given us His Holy Spirit. (1 Thessalonians 4:3–8)

---

[3] Sanctification—think of the word *sanctuary*; it comes from the Latin *sanctus*, which means *holy*. *Sanctification* is God's will for his people, that we become all the time more fit as servants of God. He saves sinful people, so, from the start, we are *not at all* fit to be ministers of God, servants of God! But that is how He is glorified, by saving people who do not deserve it, displaying His amazing mercy and love. And then He is glorified by these sinful people that He has saved being changed to be more like Him—and that is called *sanctification*. After he has saved us, we are commanded to pursue sanctification, to become better servants, to be more like Him, to become less sinful and more holy (sanctified) all the time.

God calls all of us to holiness, and when we are involved in sexual sin, there is "deadness" in our souls. We are pulled to the flesh and away from the Holy Spirit.

> For the flesh lusts against the Spirit, and the Spirit against the flesh; and these are contrary to one another, so that you do not do the things that you wish. (Galatians 5:17)

Since the inception of the Sexual Revolution, we have been persuaded to forget God's direction and "just do it." But God teaches us to use self-control.

> But the fruit of the Spirit is love, joy, peace, longsuffering, kindness, goodness, faithfulness, gentleness, self-control. (Galatians 5:22-23)

Jesus commanded men to not look lustfully upon a woman:.

> "You have heard that it was said to those of old, 'You shall not commit adultery.' But I say to you that whoever looks at a woman to lust for her has already committed adultery with her in his heart." (Matthew 5:27–28)

He is the one who designed our brains, and He knew that viewing pornography actually causes neuroplastic changes that could affect behavior and lead men to the most abhorrent of acts.

Pornography is widely accepted today and easy for children to access. The "what I do behind closed doors doesn't affect anyone else" rationale, that is promoted in society (including church culture), is *wrong*. God defines sin as sin, whether we think it hurts anybody else or not. But the truth is that our sin *does* hurt others, even though that's not our intention. I am surrounded by Christian families who have come apart because of one or both of the parents' involvement in pornography. It is time that we turn from the wicked ways! And the good news is that when we turn to God and repent, He is gracious and forgives, and immediately begins to work healing in our lives.

Having learned where sex education came from and how it has impacted those of us who were trained by it, there are further areas of our lives we must consider. Ask yourself:

- Am I currently dabbling in sexual sin?

- What is my home environment like? Is it free of sexual images or words? What about my music, television, computer, magazines, and books?

You've decided to provide your children with the tools to avoid sexual sin. But if your home environment is toxic because of sexual images or words, that will bring confusion to your children's minds and hearts. You want to make sure that you are living a life of purity in front of them and providing an environment that reflects Christ.

We as parents need to do the work of purity first; we need to get ourselves in shape. Consider this analogy: Flight attendants always instruct parents that if the plane should have a sudden change in air pressure, they should put the oxygen mask on themselves first, and then help their children put theirs on. Parents who are incapacitated by the lack of oxygen are of no help to their children!

The Sexual Revolution has incapicated a generation of parents. Sexual sin has wrought havoc, inside and outside of the church. We were the first generation to have been exposed to sex education; and many, upon being indoctrinated with that "sexual identity", went down dark paths we never dreamed we would travel—whether it be fornication, abortion,

It is time for our generation of parents to get healthy and put on the oxygen mask of God's Word so we, in turn, can help the next generation avoid the immoral disasters that we have had to endure.

(Image credit: Juliane Liebermann.)

pornography addiction, homosexuality, gender confusion, or any of the sexual sins God forbids.

I liken God's Word to the oxygen mask in the depressurized airplane.

*We are dying from the lack of God's direction.* Our families are falling apart and our nation is crumbling in every area.

It is time for our generation of parents to get healthy and put on the oxygen mask of God's Word so we, in turn, can help the next generation avoid the immoral disasters that we have had to endure.

In Ezekiel 37, God brings the prophet to a valley where some terrible slaughter has occurred long in the past, that is full of dry bones. And then He has him prophesy over the dry bones. The Holy Spirit fills the valley, the bones come together, the bodies are repaired, and these individuals become "an exceedingly great army" for the Lord![4] I can't help but think when reading this account: *How many Christians have been slain by sexual sin?*

There are so many who have not taken their sins to the cross, repented, and then left them there. When those sins rise up like zombies in our hearts, we may have to do this again and again! Satan seems to like to remind us of our past failures and whisper in our ears, "You made a mistake that you can never turn back from," and we seem to take those sins and put them in our backpacks to weigh us down throughout our lives. The truth is that you *can* turn back from any and every sin. Our Lord has promised that if we confess our sin, He who is able will forgive our sins and *cleanse us from all unrighteousness.*

> But if we walk in the light as He is in the light, we have fellowship with one another, and the blood of Jesus Christ His Son cleanses us from all sin. If we say that we have no sin, we deceive ourselves, and the truth is not in us. If we confess our sins, He is faithful and just to forgive us our sins and to cleanse us from all unrighteousness. (1 John 1:7–9)

> Then behold, they brought to Him a paralytic lying on a bed. When Jesus saw their faith, He said to the paralytic, "Son, be of good cheer; your sins are forgiven you." (Matthew 9:2)

[4] Ezekiel 37:10.

Jesus is the sacrificial Lamb of God...

> The next day John saw Jesus coming toward him, and said, "Behold! The Lamb of God who takes away the sin of the world!" (John 1:29)

Who died on that cross...

> ...Christ died for our sins according to the Scriptures. (1 Corinthians 15:3)

To cover all sin...

> ...and He died for all, that those who live should live no longer for themselves, but for Him who died for them and rose again. (2 Corinthians 5:15)

So don't let Satan keep you down!

> Therefore submit to God. Resist the devil and he will flee from you. (James 4:7)

> [But now, thus says the Lord,]
> "Do not remember the former things,
> Nor consider the things of old.
> Behold, I will do a new thing,
> Now it shall spring forth;
> Shall you not know it?
> I will even make a road in the wilderness
> And rivers in the desert." (Isaiah 43:18-19)

## Remember: More Is Caught than Is Taught!

> You are all sons of light and sons of the day. We are not of the night or of darkness. Therefore, let us not sleep, as others do, but let us watch and be sober. (1 Thessalonians 5:11)

Chapter 2

# Tip 2: We Want Our Children to Be Morally Innocent, but not Naïve

That we should no longer be children tossed to and fro and carried about with every wind of doctrine, by the trickery of men, in the cunning craftiness of deceitful plotting. (Ephesians 4:14)

In 1997, with the thimbleful of knowledge I'd newly acquired about the sex education curriculum we were using at our local Lutheran school, it was time for truth telling in the Sex Education Curriculum Review Committee there. I was given the opportunity to talk about Alfred Kinsey, his pseudo-science, and his influence on the *Learning About Sex* series we were using.

Although I was an experienced educator, and the presentation only fifteen minutes long, it was exhausting—mentally, physically, and spiritually. I realized that where the Apostle Paul says that "we do not wrestle against flesh and blood, but against principalities, against powers, against the rulers of the darkness of this age, against spiritual hosts of wickedness in the heavenly places," that he meant business![1] I recognized that my exhaustion was coming, not from any physical cause which I could discern, but from a spiritual battle.

As I brought my portion of the Review Committee work to a conclusion, a committee member responded in anger at the possibility that we had gotten it wrong for so many years. "How," he loudly protested, "Is it possible that the curriculum, believed and used for the last thirty years, could be wrong?" He was more offended at a whistle blower than that children were being robbed of their innocence.

This man had a personal and heartfelt reason for his objections. As a youth, he had suffered embarrassment in the boys' locker room, when the other boys' talk turned to the graphic details of sexual intimacy, which he did not yet know. In other words, there was dirty talk, and the other boys mocked him for his innocence. Years later, he wanted to ensure that other Christian boys did not have to suffer such deep wounds.

These concerns hit directly upon our next Tip: We Want Our Children to Be Morally Innocent, but Not Naïve.

We must not ignore the curiosity that grows in them as they approach maturity and make the mistake of giving them no information, or make them ignorant of information they are naturally gaining. When parents, the most trusted people in our children's lives, don't guide their thinking, we are eroding their trust in us. It is important both to inform our children and maintain their moral innocence.

Is there a way to do both? The answer is a resounding *Yes!* It is called the Indirect Method.

Sex education uses an approach called the Graphic Direct Method, which robs children of their innocence. When the Graphic Direct Method is used, children are taught the details of the act and shown graphic pictures, to the end that they are no longer morally innocent about sex. Their senses will be on high alert when they hear a reference to the genitals or the act. *They will be reminded of those graphic words or pictures every time there is any reference to sex.*

---

[1] Ephesians 6:12.

Before the age of Kinsey, children were given "the birds and the bees" talk. The Indirect Method uses the approach of talking about God's life process through that—the flowers, the birds, and the bees. If we use this approach with our children, we can teach them everything they need to know, without robbing them of their moral innocence. As a matter of fact, their moral innocence can actually insulate them from the graphic world around them! Let me give you a personal life example:

Our children were 12, 10, and 9 years old, and my husband had just picked them up from school. While waiting at a stoplight the kids said, "Dad, look, there's a naked woman!" My husband turned around in alarm, thinking there was a naked woman running around in traffic. But instead he was saddened to see a jeep full of teenage boys, holding a *Playboy* centerfold up to the window for the children to see.

My husband responded with grace and wisdom, by saying to the children, "Kids, turn away. That is not appropriate." (What an excellent example for how to handle that kind of situation!) But as they drove away, my oldest son said to my husband, "Dad, she was not naked; she had on black underpants." My husband had to think for a moment... and then he realized what he was talking about. My son had never seen a picture of a naked woman before, and he had no other frame of reference, so his mind went to something he *did* know—a covered area equals black underpants. His innocence had protected him from what he had seen.

There is another great example given by Gary Ezzo in the video series, *Protecting the Innocence of Children*. Gary shares a story related to him by the mother of a five-year-old boy, who had returned home after his morning in Kindergarten. There had been a speaker that day who had spoken to the children about HIV and AIDS. Horrified at what her child might have been exposed to, this mother asked her son what he had learned. His reply was, "Something about that when we come to an *intersection*, we are supposed to have a *condo*." Again, this child went to something he knew, which was *intersection* and not *intercourse*, and *condo* instead of *condom*. The Indirect Method informs children, while insulating them from evil.

An important element of the Indirect Method is understanding that giving knowledge to our children is a progressive task. Just like with math, history, and English, a five-year-old child doesn't need the same level of information about his sexuality that he will need when he is sixteen. Despite what "the experts" say, parents need not give their children graphic images they are not yet ready to handle.

Dr. Miriam Grossman explains how children respond to information they are not mature enough to understand:

> A young child's ability to think logically is limited. [In his thinking, he moves from the concrete to the abstract. Adults, on the other hand, think from the abstract to the concrete.] His understanding of the world is magical and egocentric. Why did his uncle leave? Because little Johnny wished he would. Why is it raining? So Johnny can wear his new boots. He devises his own theories to explain reality, based on his experiences. Providing facts that are beyond his experience—his uncle had a heart attack and went to the hospital; it's raining because ocean water evaporates... will likely be ineffective. They will sound bizarre, even impossible, to him. The result: confusion.
>
> The sex ed oligarchy must realize that a young child has his own theories about where babies come from, and he will cling to them regardless of how carefully and deliberately parents follow their instructions. Large amounts of unexpected information that cannot be easily assimilated into previously-held beliefs can be distressing to children.[2]

Grossman reiterates what we parents understand—that the development of a child's mind from purely concrete thinking to abstract reasoning is a slow, natural process which, if rushed, results in confusion.

It is ok to feel awkward about delivering sexually explicit material to your children. If we feel this awkwardness, we should hesitate in going further. Why? Because we are robbing our children of the innocence of their childhood when we follow the dictates of our society. That hesitation you are feeling is a God-given alarm in your spirit, warning you against doing something that will harm your child.

---

[2] Miriam Grossman, M.D., *You're Teaching My Child What?: A Physician Exposes the Lies of Sex Ed and How They Harm Your Child* (Washington D.C.: Regency Publishing, Inc., 2009), 30.

God, who does not change, has given us a way to communicate sexual truths to our children without having to use the Graphic Direct Method. We will discuss the methods of communicating in more detail in the next few Tips. But first, here is one last example of the beauty of keeping children morally innocent, but not naïve:

In the spring of 2000, our five-year-old daughter was admiring a lovely display of tulips in full bloom, with several little friends. I was standing behind her with the other moms, when my daughter proceeded to tell all of her friends the story of the flower and how it had a mommy part and a daddy part, and how when the two got together a baby flower was made. The other mothers and I just smiled as we looked at these morally innocent children, our hearts made a little warmer by this glimpse of God's goodness. But just think—had my daughter been giving the graphic talk to her little friends at that moment, that scene would have taken on a different tone!

Let's let children be children.

## **Remember:** We Want Our Children to Be Morally Innocent, but not Naïve!

> ...but I want you to be wise in what is good, and simple concerning evil. (Romans 16:19b)

# TIP 3: APPROACH THE TOPIC WITH MODESTY

...and the parts that are unpresentable are treated with modesty. (1 Corinthians 12:23b, NIV)

Ask yourself: *How do I feel about giving my child the "sex talk"?* Are you dreading it? Does it make you uncomfortable?

Why is there discomfort in talking with our children about sex? The sex experts will say, "Get over it," or something like, "You are too old-fashioned, too Victorian in your thinking, and you just need to get with the times." They will encourage you to push those feelings aside "for the good of your children," and give your little ones the Graphic Direct sex talk.

I propose that this inhibition is as natural as the sky is blue, and there is nothing to get over. Talking graphically about sex with your children *is* uncomfortable; your response is natural and healthy, because the graphic approach is *not biblical.* Using Kinsey's method robs your children of their modesty and leaves them more vulnerable to pornography. As we learned in Tip 2, those inhibitions are your *conscience*, warning you against doing something that will harm your precious little ones.

Twenty years ago, at founding of The Matthew XVIII Group ministry, my objectives were to reveal the truth to parents and awaken them to the graphic content of the *Learning About Sex* curriculum being used in many Christian schools and churches. The claims that this curriculum was "Christ-centered" and "Bible-based" were false. It had detailed pictures of naked males and females as well as a graphically worded description of sexual intercourse, including how the body parts fit together.

At every parent meeting, I would request parents' participation. I would ask a volunteer to read selected passaged from the curriculum aloud. No parent ever felt comfortable with my request. Every time, without exception, each parent felt it would be "too embarrassing" to read aloud. But somehow this was seen as acceptable for our 8-year-olds. This I found to be extremely revealing. Why did these parents find this uncomfortable?

I realized that, in scripture, God never mentions a man or woman's private parts, nor the act of marriage in detail. This drove me to consider, *Why?* Why was there no mention? Was this intentional on God's part? Was it possible that God has placed in our hearts a natural prohibition?

I sought out Dr. Chris Mitchell, author of the *Song of Songs Concordia Commentary* and consultant for the *1 Corinthians Commentary*. I asked him if I was interpreting 1 Corinthians 12:23b correctly (see the opening of this chapter); was this scripture talking about sexuality and our private parts? He verified that my understanding was correct, and that this was consistent with other scriptures! He said that God was intentionally modeling a tremendous amount of modesty for us throughout the Bible. For example, he explained in Song of Songs (which, lately, is being called the "Bible's hot book on sex" by some ill-informed scholars), Solomon describes his wife's body in detail... but notice that Solomon skips the genital area.[1]

> How beautiful are your **feet** in sandals, O prince's daughter! The curves of your **thighs** are like jewels, the work of the hands of a skillful workman, your **navel** is a rounded goblet; it lacks no blended beverage. Your **waist** is a heap of wheat set about with lilies. (Song of Songs 7:1–2)

---

[1] Dr. Christopher Mitchell is the author of *The Song of Songs Commentary* published by Concordia Publishing House, and he is a seminary professor at Concordia St. Louis Seminary for the Lutheran Church-Missouri Synod.

Dr. Mitchell also went on to say that the genitals were considered such a holy, procreative area, that they were treated with a tremendous amount of modesty.

The scriptures are replete with examples of this.

> Now Adam *knew* Eve his wife.[2]
>
> And when Shechem... saw [Dinah], he took her, and *lay with* her, and *defiled* her.[3]
>
> You shall not *lie with* a male as with a woman.[4]
>
> [David] *lay with* [Bathsheba]...[5]
>
> It is actually reported that there is *sexual immorality* among you... —that a man *has* his father's wife![6]
>
> ...because of *sexual immorality*, let each man *have* his own wife, and let each woman *have* her own husband. Let the husband *render to his wife the affection due her*, and likewise also the wife to her husband. The wife does not have authority over her own body, but the husband does. And likewise the husband does not have authority over his own body, but the wife does. Do not *deprive one another* except with consent for a time, that you may give yourselves to fasting and prayer; and *come together again* so that Satan does not tempt you because of your lack of self-control.[7]

God, in His Word, uses euphemistic language to talk about these things. In His wonderful wisdom, He tells us everything we need to know about this important area of our lives, yet in such a way that when children read these scriptures, their innocence is not stolen away.

Parents at my meetings felt uncomfortable reading aloud the description of intercourse in the children's sex education series, because the Holy Spirit values modesty, as demonstrated in scripture.

---

[2] Genesis 4:1.

[3] Genesis 34:1 (KJV).

[4] Leviticus 18:22.

[5] 2 Samuel 11:4.

[6] 1 Corinthians 5:1.

[7] 1 Corinthians 7:2–5.

Parent, you do not have to overcome that modesty to talk to your children about God's life process. To the contrary, you are to embrace it. Know the Graphic Direct Method is not biblical.

Even nature itself teaches that it is not natural to teach our children the graphic details about procreation. Do we have to teach our children how to use their eyes? Their ears? Do we have to teach them how to pick things up with their hands? Goodness, we don't even have to teach our children how to walk, balancing upright!

Three times in Song of Songs, God gives us the warning, "Do not stir up nor awaken love until it pleases."[8]

*The Roby Family, or, Battling with the World,* by A.L.O.E., London: T. Nelson & Sons, 1870.

This understanding was once a part of our culture. Prior to the Sexual Revolution, literature reflected that modesty. One of my hobbies has become collecting antique books on parenting and purity. In these books I have found the same biblical approach: modesty and caution were always used.

In one book from 1912, the author addresses a parent who "thinks that the way to protect her daughter of fourteen from falling into sexual danger is to tell her everything in detail." The author replies:

> To this mother I say, with renewed emphasis, that *information does not protect.* I would be extremely careful in what I said to a girl of fourteen. To "tell her everything in detail," as this mother suggests, might be to put her in a place of great danger. We must remember that, just at this period of her life, the creative forces of

[8] Song of Songs 2:7, 3:5, 8:4.

> her being are receiving a new impulse. Not only are new powers awakening in her body, but in her mind as well. Especially is her imagination increasing greatly in its activity, and is prone to follow any suggestion made to it along the line of this new process of development. And therein lies the danger of the plan this mother proposes.[9] (Emphasis added.)

The parents of a century ago were also struggling with what to say to their children about modesty. This author did not have the decades of statistical research that we now have, showing what telling kids "every detail" about sex has done to them. But she did have the Bible's clear teaching on the matter. As the Bible gave this author wisdom about modesty, it provides the same wisdom to us.

Another example of modesty comes from Dr. Mary Ries Melendy, a female physician who taught in 1904, under the heading "Sexual Organs are to be Kept Sacred":

> God made them [the sex organs], and they are the most sacred of all, for to them is given the honor and privilege, under right conditions, after marriage, of creating life.[10]

In the 1990s, looking back on the changes that had taken place since those days, the authors of the *RSVP America Training Manual* well stated:

> Sex was once hidden out of recognition of its power as well as a sense of modesty and respect for privacy. What was once sacred is now, in the name of science and freedom, being taught as "safe sex" and sex education in public, private, and parochial school classrooms.[11]

No parent who is training his child in purity would find it appropriate to show that child a picture of a *Playboy* centerfold, or to read an excerpt from a trashy romance novel. Modesty tells us to protect our children. Unfortunately most of sex education focuses on the act and the genitals, violating childen's moral innocence, their modesty. It is important

---

[9] Mrs. Woodallen Chapman, *How Shall I Tell My Child* (New York: Fleming H. Revell Co., 1912), 50.

[10] Mary Ries Melendy, M.D., *Vivilore: The Pathway to Mental and Physical Perfection* (W.R. Vansant Pub., 1904), 295.

[11] Judith Reisman, Ph.D.; Dennis Jerrard, Ph.D.; Colonel Ronald Ray U.S.M.C.; & Eunice Ray; *RSVP America Training Manual* (Crestwood, KY: First Principles, Inc., 1996), 4.

to those who promote Kinsey's "science" to *remove* modesty; they are working to devalue the family and to groom children for sex outside of marriage.

Modesty is a standard given to us by God. He models it for us in His Word. He encourages us to remain pure in our thoughts, words, and deeds (Psalm 119). If we take away modesty from children, hence opening them up to sexual sin, God has a few words to say to us about that:

> Whoever causes one of these little ones who believe in Me to sin, it would be better for him if a millstone were hung around his neck, and he were drowned in the depth of the sea. Woe to the world because of offenses! For offenses must come, but woe to that man by whom the offense comes. (Matthew 18:6-7)

In my training it was apparent that modesty was not the goal of Planned Parenthood, or of those funding sex education (the pornography industry). SIECUS was determined to reprogram their trainees by taking away any modesty we had toward the subject of sex. Their rationale was that if we were no longer modest about these terms, we could then encourage the children no longer to be modest about these terms.

I was disappointed to learn that Christian publishing companies are using the very same resources from SIECUS, Planned Parenthood, and the porn industry that the world uses. *Having trusted these Christian publishers, had I as a parent unintentionally violated my children's modesty?*

*The Giant Killer, or, The Battle which All Must Fight*, by A.L.O.E., London: T. Nelson & Sons, 1868.

As I came to understand biblical truth, and I looked back at the instructions I'd learned from the "experts" encouraging parents to teach our children "correct anatomical terms", I realized I had been in error. What was my next step? I went to my children and apologized; I acted quickly to change. I immediately switched to a more modest approach.

The Barna Group recently confirmed that our current methods of sex education rob our children of their modesty. In a recent study, they found that our current generation of young people believe that *not recycling their trash is more morally wrong than viewing pornography*.[12] How can this be?

Many people today see nothing wrong with viewing others engaged in sex acts. Once modesty is removed through sex education, the easy next step is to slip into viewing pornography, because *sex education, in the way it is designed, is pornography.* And now, pornography is widely accepted and easily accessible.

In 1996, the Catholic community responded to the connection between sex education and sex stimulation in their informational booklet, *Parents and the Purity of Children*:

> Pope Pius in his encyclical "On Chaste Wedlock," in 1930, warned against any type of (sex) education helping people to "sin subtly." Much of our dramatic presentations which are defended as "realistic" are really pandering to the sexual prurience, and tumescence-seeking of easily stirred children, adolescents, and adults.... Sexological research and its application in science (as in sex education) and art are notorious for the seduction of the parent, teacher, lawyer, physician, psychiatrist, social worker, nun and priest.[13]

Several years ago, as I was uncovering the origins of the *Learning About Sex* series, a call from a Lutheran pastor confirmed my concerns. He was attempting to challenge the use of this series in the elementary school (grades K–8) associated with his church. The curriculum had been taught at this school for over thirty years. This pastor shared that of all the congregations he had worked in, he had never seen more sexual sin than there was in this congregation. He believed that as a result of the exposure to explicit sexual information through the *Learning About Sex* series,

---

[12] http://www.christianitydaily.com/articles/7618/20160121/comprehensive-survey-porn-phenomenon-reveals-general-christian-population-struggling.htm

[13] Rev. H. Vernon Sattler, C.Ss.R., PhD., *Parents and the Purity of Children* (St. Louis: Central Bureau, 1996), 40–41.

many adults in their community, who were once taught the curriculum as youth, were involved in unhealthy sexual practices.

He told of a specific incident that had occurred at his church, which demonstrated the connection between sex education and pornography. The summer after an eighth grade boy had graduated from their school, he broke into the school and accessed porn on the school's computers. You may ask, "Why did he go there to view porn?" This Pastor believes it was because this school was where his modesty had been taken away. The school was where he had been sexually stimulated, and where he had been exposed year after year, for eight years, to the procreative act, which he should have been morally protected from instead of overexposed to.

*There is a huge connection between sex education and pornography, and it's time more parents and teachers understand this.*

But when you use God's model of modesty when talking to your children, it will be natural, it will be progressive (growing in detail as they grow and mature), and it won't violate their moral innocence.

## **Remember:** Approach the Topic with Modesty!

> As for God, His way is perfect; the word of the Lord is proven; He is a shield to all who trust in him. (Psalm 18:30)

Chapter 4

# Tip 4: Identity Matters

But you are a chosen generation, a royal priesthood, a holy nation, His own special people, that you may proclaim the praises of Him who called you out of darkness into His marvelous light. (1 Peter 2:9)

Is it a coincidence that, in 1962 and 1963, two revolutionary Supreme Court decisions removed God entirely from the schools, and then in the very next year, 1964, sex education was put into the schools? You remember: The first decision in 1962 declared that prayer was banned from public schools, and the second decision in 1963 removed the reading of God's Word from the public schools, clearing a path for SIECUS to bring sex education into the schools to fill that void.

Every child asks, *Who am I? Why am I here?* The Bible had answered those questions for American children, but now they would be taught that they were sexual beings, existing for sexual pleasure.

We have learned that it is important to direct the thinking of the children if we want to affect social change in the future. We as parents need to capitalize on this truth, reminding our children of Whose they are, rather than allowing a philosophy opposed to Christ to capture their thinking.

Sex is part of God's design; it is not uncommon to watch the Liar and Deceiver take one of God's most precious gifts and distort it. Through the vehicle of SIECUS, children were introduced to the act of intimacy that God designed to be saved for marriage.

What do kids need to grow up healthy and productive? What did experts of previous decades advise? In the first half of the 20th century, child development experts did not identify knowledge of sex and sexuality as a prime childhood needs. Theorists Jean Piaget, Carl Rogers, Abraham Maslow, and B.F. Skinner concentrated on individual and group skills such as: learning to reason, submitting to authority, moral thinking, task achievement, self-actualization (fulfillment of one's potential), mutual cooperation, and social interaction. These were seen as the child's major developmental objectives.[1]

But Alfred Kinsey did not consult with child development specialists when doing his own "research".[2] We now know that he interviewed pedophiles who had raped children.[3] This information has been verified via interviews with these pedophiles; those "doing research" were instructed to use stopwatches to time what they claimed were children's orgasms during intercourse.[4] It is this "research" that has led us, as a society, to believe that children are *sexual beings* who should be trained on how to handle their sexuality. Now children are seen as sexual beings capable of engaging in, expressing preferences about, and enjoying sex—along with all of its trappings—from a very young age. As a result, we as a society have come to see our identities as sexual, and not as we are truly created—as precious image bearers of God.[5]

Michael Balfour, researcher and author stated:

> [When] someone in public life can persuade enough people to act on the assumption that his interpretation is valid, he can so

---

[1] Michael Craven, "What is wrong with Sex Education" (Center for Christ and Culture, January 16, 2008).

[2] Alfred Kinsey, Wardell Pomeroy, and Clyde Martin, *Sexual Behavior in the Human Male* (Philadelphia: W.B. Saunders Company, 1948), 175–181. Kinsey describes orgasms in young children as "sobbing, sometimes with an abundance of tears, and afflicted with 'extreme trembling' collapse, and sometimes fainting." Kinsey also wrote that the children "enjoy the experience" but many "fight away the partner."

[3] Judith Reisman, *Sexual Sabotage: How One Mad Scientist Unleashed a Plague or Corruption and Contagion on America* (Washington D.C.: World Net Daily, 2010), 24.

[4] Alfred Kinsey, Wardell Pomeroy, and Clyde Martin, *Sexual Behavior in the Human Male* (Philadelphia: W.B. Saunders Company, 1948), 180–181.

[5] Genesis 1:27.

> influence the character of the future as to make it consistent with his predictions.[6]

Ever heard of a self-fulfilling prophecy?

Believing that children are sexual from birth and can be sexually active changed everything. This lie has affected us in many ways.

**Schools** were now faced with the task of teaching children how to handle their *sexuality*, not simply educating them in reading, writing, and arithmetic.

> As soon as it was established, SIECUS became a super-salesman for sex education. Soon after, schools began talking sex education.[7]

**Legislators** were trained to look at a sexual predator with sympathy, hence reducing their sentences from imprisonment for life or the death penalty to being *therapeutically* managed and living in our neighborhoods.

> The sometimes-extreme seductiveness of a young female is a factor which has no place in the law, but it certainly affects motivation. Even at the age of four or five, this seductiveness may be so powerful as to overwhelm the adult into committing the offense. The affair is therefore not always the result of the adult's aggression; *often the young female is the initiator and seducer.* (Emphasis added.)[8]

**Medical personnel** were taught that if children are sexual beings, they must be interviewed separately from their parents, so the doctor can get a clear picture of their sexual activity. Vaccines are now administered to children to protect against sexual diseases, such as Hepatitis B and Human Papilloma Virus (HPV), in the belief that children are capable of intercourse at any time, yet not mature enough to practice "safe-sex" or remain pure until marriage.

---

[6] Michael Balfour, *Propaganda in War, 1939–1945: Organizations, Policies and Publics in Britain and Germany* (London: Routledge and Kegan Paul, 1979), 424.

[7] Gloria Lentz, *Raping Our Children: The Sex Education Scandal* (New Rochelle, N.Y.: Arlington House, 1972), 21.

[8] Ralph Slovenko and C. Philips, "Psychosexuality and the Criminal Law," *Vanderbilt Law Review*, Vol. 15 (1962), 809.

**Christian churches and schools** were faced with the challenge of taking this new "science" and developing "Christian Sex Education" programs using scripture meshed with Kinsey's fraudulent data. One of the most popular of these programs rationalized the need to talk graphically with kids about sex:

> The famous Kinsey reports are more specific. His study reveals that by the age of 20, 75% of males had premarital coitus. Of the women marrying for the first time between 16 and 20, 47% were no longer virgins.[9]

**Parents** were confronted with the task talking graphically to their kids about sex, and because many found it uncomfortable, they either remained silent or relied on the schools and churches to do it. At the same time, sex education experts made clear their belief that parents were ill-equipped to teach their children accurately about sex. Past president of SIECUS, Dr. Harold Lief, had this to say:

> Most parents are so d*** anxious about this [sex education] that if they attempted to teach it, all they do is transfer their own anxiety to the kids. A lot of parents are so hung up about sex that their own repressive and suppressive mechanisms just increase their kids' guilt and anxiety. The parents who scream "let the parents do it" are just the ones who will stir up all kinds of harmful emotions in their children. They think they'll do a good job—but I doubt it.[10]

Words and images are powerful. Sexual words and images are even more powerful; if you have ever viewed pornography or read trashy romance novels or even watched an R-rated movie, you well know what I am talking about. Those who developed sex education came up with a way to convey sexual words and images to children, the *SAR Technique* (Sexual Attitude Restructuring) that we learned about in Part I. The goal of this technique is to break down all modesty and reshape attitudes toward sexuality, as well as to train a healthy brain to consider deviant sexual mores. Leading expert on Kinsey, Judith Reisman, wrote:

---

[9] Erwin J. Kolb, *Parents Guide to Christian Conversation about Sex* (St. Louis: Concordia Publishing, 1967), 20.

[10] Gloria Lentz, *Raping Our Children: The Sex Education Scandal* (New Rochelle, NY: Arlington House, 1972), 165.

> The neurochemical impact of sexualized media, whether commercial or educative, upon children's nascent brains, minds, and memories, is producing a new breed of children, hence a new breed of adults and a new type of society.[11]

Reisman later went on to report:

> Using a "Graffiti Board" to desensitize students to "dirty words," sex educators taught children about nudity, adolescent pregnancy, masturbation, abortion, homosexuality, contraception, divorce, group sex, and extramarital relations. By 1973, "Thanks to Kinsey, every form of deviance is promulgated throughout our schools," reported psychiatrist Charles Socarides, MD.[12]

Today, in the ever-evolving field of sex education, a new priority is being promoted: putting doubt into children's minds regarding their very gender. To compare, when we taught that a child's identity and purpose was found in the God who created him, there was no confusion that each person was born either male or female. But when a child's identity is found in his being a "sexual being", we have opened Pandora's box to endless confusion.

Here's a recent example of what children are being taught, from a book being used in schools at the Kindergarten level:

> When we are born, a doctor or midwife calls us boy or girl because of what we look like on the outside. They choose a word or label (usually boy or girl, or male or female) to describe our bodies. But that's based on our outside, our cover, and who they think we are. What about our whole body, inside and out? What about who *we* think we are?[13]

Another example of a suggested identity comes in the "Christian" *Learning About Sex* series:

---

[11] Judith Reisman, PhD, *Kinsey, Crimes and Consequences* (Crestwood, KY: The Institute for Media Education, 2000), 174.

[12] Judith Reisman, *Sexual Sabotage: How One Mad Scientist Unleashed a Plague or Corruption and Contagion on America* (Washington D.C.: World Net Daily, 2010), 183.

[13] Cory Silverberg and Fiona Smyth, *Sex is a Funny Word: A Book about Bodies, Feelings, and YOU* (Seven Stories Press, 2015), 81.

> Scientific study of homosexuality [i.e. Kinsey's "science"] is comparatively new and relatively unknown. It is estimated that about a third [Kinsey's statistic was 37%] of all males have had some homosexual experience at some point... Many young people experience homosexual attraction to people of their own age as well as to older or younger people... *Most of us cannot escape homosexual temptations*, but homosexual practice involves choosing this pattern of action. (Emphasis added.)[14]

We have an epidemic of youth who are declaring they are gay, and many adults don't understand where this is coming from. In her report titled, "Crafting Gay Children: An Inquiry into the Abuse of Vulnerable Youth via Government Schooling & Mainstream Media," Dr. Judith Reisman reveals how our children are being recruited into dangerous lifestyles:

> Sexuality philosophers like Gilbert Herdt, the editor of "Gay and Lesbian Youth," defines adult homosexuals (not bisexuals) as "coaches" and "guides," who help children overcome their heterosexual victim status by "coming out" into homosexuality. Protected by federal and state law, homosexual "guides" teaching "tolerance", "sexual diversity", and such, frighten susceptible child audiences with Kinsey's "scientific" claim that, "at least one in ten of you are gay." Objectors are labeled "homophobic" fascists. Supporters are rewarded with love, approval and inspiring encouragement to be "gay and proud."[15]

Reisman continues:

> Children (labeled "initiates" as in prostitution or religion), are weaned from their "old fashioned" parents, first into a self-affirming semi-secret group, then by collective socialization into a "gay" cultural system (a form of cult).[16]

Alfred Kinsey's "science" has been used to legalize all that had been illegal when America's laws were still based on the Bible; and those who encour-

---

[14] Elmer Witt, *Life Can Be Sexual* (part of the original *Learning About Sex* series) (Concordia Publishing House, 1967), 44.

[15] Judith Reisman, PhD., "Crafting Gay Children: An Inquiry into the Abuse of Vulnerable Youth via Government Schooling & Mainstream Media" (Crestwood, KY: The Institute for Media Education, 2000), 18.

[16] Ibid., 19.

age homosexuality have especially benefitted from it. Psychotherapist Edward Eichel, with M.A. in Human Sexuality, speaks of the benefits, as he sees them to be, of Kinsey's influence:

> The objective of Kinsey-type programming is to change the concept of the family or "de-normalize" the heterosexual nuclear family. If you look to the statement of pedophile Theo Sanford, he said that if children could be weaned away from the nuclear family, they can then form emotional attachments with others beyond the family... With the systematic destruction of the family with a mother and father in it and with the family break-ups that are occurring, it is an opportune time.[17]

Eichel was not the first to promote the correlation between the removal of the influence of the family with the attainment of new social goals. This type of thinking was also present with the Hitler Youth and under the creative social transformation of giants like Stalin and Lenin. They knew that by altering loyalties and changing identities, new laws according to their own philosophies would be written, and then acted upon. This is what is driving the push to change our children's identities.

Why is it so dangerous to give children a sexual identity? Why are many in the LGBTQ community so intent on encouraging children to consider an identity based on their sexuality above all other accomplishments? Why does Planned Parenthood devote the month of October to encouraging parents to talk to their kids about sex, hence employing the parents in the task of giving their children a sexual identity? Why is all of this a problem? Linda Bartlett summarizes it beautifully:

> It matters how we identify ourselves. If we are mistaken about our identity, we will be mistaken about our purpose, behavior, and choices.[18]

Once a student is given that sexual identity—whether it be straight or gay—their purpose will not be to follow Christ, minister to the lost and hurting on this earth, or to help others to come to know Christ; it will be

---

[17] Excerpt from the video "The Children of Table 34," distributed by the Family Research Council (1998).

[18] Linda Bartlett, *The Failure of Sex Education in the Church: Mistaken Identity, Compromised Purity: Questions and Answers for Christian Dialogue* (Iowa Falls, IA: Titus 2 for Life, 2014), 28.

to pursue sexual pleasure, and fight for sexual rights to be legal, and suppress those who hold a different opinion. Dr. Miriam Grossman writes:

> Once kids believe that sexuality is "who they are", "their entire selves" from womb to tomb, the idea that it's an appetite in need of restraint makes little sense. And the notion of waiting years for the right time and person sounds irrational. Why restrain "who you are"? Why wait for "your entire self"? Couldn't that be unhealthy?[19]

The choices children make once they embrace this identity will only harm them, because that false identity ignores several realities:

- That having more than one sex partner can put them in harm's way to contract diseases—some of which could kill them.[20]
- That aboring a baby is actually murdering one's own child.
- That aborting a baby also causes many of those potential parents to suffer depression and emotional distress.[21]
- That engaging in sodomy, an act God never intended the body to go through, can cause venereal diseases, cancers, and even death.[22]
- That to bear a child without a father to help protect and provide for the child means this child is more likely to grow up in poverty and repeat the cycle of having sex outside of marriage.[23]
- That any type of sexual activity outside of God's design can bring physical, spiritual, and emotional death.

---

[19] Miriam Grossman, M.D., *You're Teaching My Child What?: A Physician Exposes the Lies of Sex Ed and How They Harm Your Child* (Washington D.C.: Regency Publishing, Inc., 2009), 29.

[20] For more information, please read *Epidemic: How Teen Sex is Killing our Kids*, by Meg Meeker, M.D (Washington, D.C.: LifeLine Press, 2002).

[21] For more information, please read *Forbidden Grief: The Unspoken Pain of Abortion*, by Theresa Burke, Ph.D. (Acorn Books: 2000).

[22] For more information, please read *The Health Hazards of Homosexuality: What the Medical and Psychological Research Reveals*, by Paul Church, M.D. (MassResistance Press, 2017).

[23] Patrick Fagan, "Social Stability in the United States," https://www.catholiceducation.org/en/controversy/population-control/social-stability-in-the-united-states.html.

There was a time not long ago when divorce, out-of-wedlock pregnancy, venereal disease, and even suicide rates were low. *The Christian church influenced the culture with biblical values, and the family was recognized as a married man and woman with whatever number of children God chose to give them.* Having numerous children was once looked upon as a blessing. We have drifted far from this norm very quickly... in only sixty years!

In an attempt to counter the onslaught of sex education programs that have been pouring into the schools, some well-meaning individuals came up with "abstinence" programs. At first, these programs promoted abstinence until marriage in a modest way. However, many abstinence programs today have evolved into sex education programs—explaining the act in detail and showing pictures of diseased genitals to students of all ages. There are serious problems with this approach.

> Abstinence says, "I must wait for sex until marriage." Purity says, "I don't have to wait to be the woman (or man) God created me to be." Abstinence says, "Because we are sexual beings, I must be cautious with the opposite sex." Purity says, "Because we are *persons* more than sexual beings, I can respect, talk to, learn from,

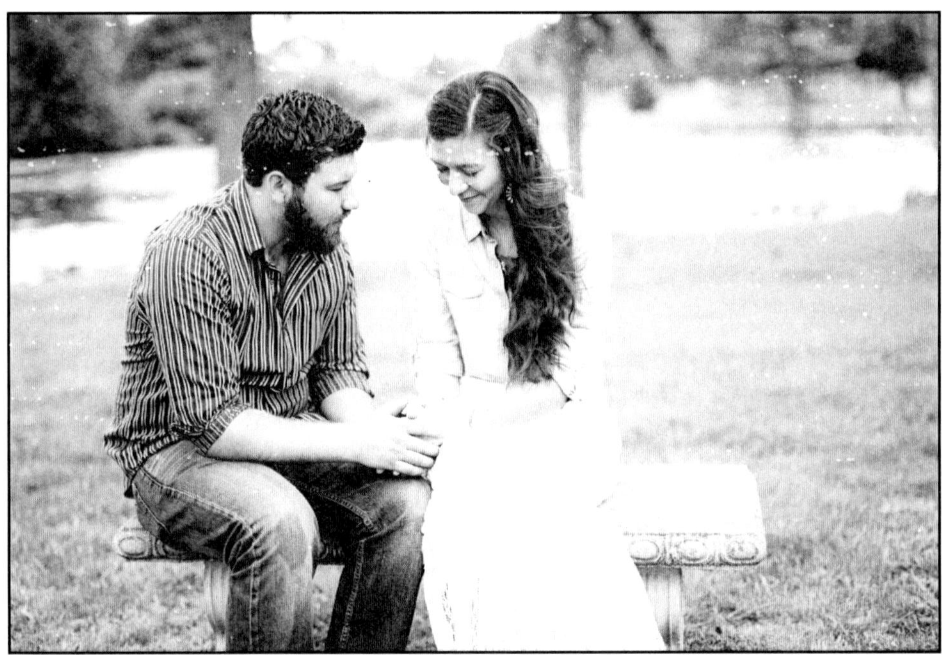

Purity always journeys toward hope with the encouragement of the Holy Spirit.
(Image credit: Shutterstock.)

> work besides, and be patient with the opposite sex." ... Purity always journeys toward hope with the encouragement of the Holy Spirit. In fact, because of Jesus Christ, we can be restored to a life of purity even after we've failed to abstain. (Emphasis added.)[24]

How can we raise up the next generation to believe, despite everything the media and schools are throwing at them, that they are made in the image of our Heavenly Father? How do we promote purity as the goal for which they should strive? God's Word is the answer!

We must stress to our children the following points:

- We are made in God's image.[25]
- We are His.[26]
- We are to be holy.[27]
- The Holy Spirit dwells within us[28] and gives us the power to turn away from evil![29]
- We are transformed through Christ Jesus![30]
- God defines biblical manhood and womanhood throughout the Bible.[31]
- We were once in the darkness, but in becoming a child of God, each of us is commanded to walk in the light.[32]
- Everything we do on earth, we are to do in the name of Jesus, giving all thanks to Him.[33]

It is important as parents to be *proactive* in training our children that who they are *is who God created them to be*. They are His image bearers. Their identity in Christ will act as a shield to protect them from the lies

---

[24] Linda Bartlett, *The Failure of Sex Education in the Church: Mistaken Identity, Compromised Purity: Questions and Answers for Christian Dialogue* (Iowa Falls, IA: Titus 2 for Life, 2014), as quoted at https://ezerwoman.blog/2015/03/20/rethinking-human-identity-and-sex-education.

[25] Genesis 1:27.

[26] Psalm 100:3.

[27] 1 Peter 1:16.

[28] Galatians 6:15, II Corinthians 5:17.

[29] Philippians 4:13.

[30] Colossians 3:10.

[31] Genesis 2, Proverbs 31, Titus 2.

[32] Ephesians 5:8.

[33] Colossians 3:17.

the world is throwing at them. Knowing who they are as God's children will influence the actions, decisions, and directions they take. Tim Tebow shared how important our identity can be in a recent interview:

> Your identity is what you get to hold onto. It's the foundation of who you are. It's not what you do. You could put your identity into sports or your girlfriend or boyfriend or a job or even your family, but none of those are going to be an identity that sustains you through everything. What's going to sustain you is a relationship with Christ. That's going to give you the strength to get through everything else you go through in your life. My significance doesn't come in what the media says about me, what type of car I drive, what type of house I have, but it comes from who I am in Christ. Then I take that same framework and I get to apply that to everyone I come in contact with. You treat people with respect because they matter to God.[34]

Right now, those who want to capture the minds of our children and give them a different identity are laying their plans, devising their traps.[35] We have a very different battle to fight than the one our parents or grandparents fought; our children will encounter peers who would entice them in many educational venues, from public school to even Sunday School.

What's more, children are seen as having power that supersedes their parents' authority, and that allows them to decide their own identity, and act upon it with impunity—that they can decide that which is morally right or wrong for themselves. Parents are being robbed of the opportunity to give our children their true identity, one based on the Truth!

Those who have been raped or molested often define themselves by these horrific experiences; some think little of themselves or feel a tremendous amount of guilt, believing that they deserved it. Some, when raped by the same gender, then grow up believing that they must be "gay." I grieve for all the children who are being sexually abused daily, and I'm thankful that through the grace of God, all of them can be healed and restored! God provides amazing tools to help in this restoration, through prayer,

---

[34] Charles Chandler, "The Testing of Tim Tebow," *Decision Magazine* (November, 2016), 32–33.

[35] Proverbs 1:10–19.

God's powerful Word, and sound biblical counseling from our older, wiser brothers and sisters in Christ.

Through the Sexual Revolution, Satan has cast many lies, luring us away from embracing God's standard of purity and holiness, with the paltry substitue of a sexual identity. Our enemy roams the earth seeking whom he can devour,[36] but we have the power of God's Word to help our children flee from sexual immorality.[37] Make sure you continue to remind your children who they are in Christ Jesus, because others are waiting in the wings to give your children a different identity—a sexual identity.

## Remember: Identity Matters!

> You are all sons of the light and sons of the day. We are not of the night nor of darkness. (1 Thessalonians 5:5)

---

[36] 1 Peter 5:8.

[37] 1 Corinthians 6:18.

Chapter 5

# Tip 5: Don't Use the S-Word (Sex!)

Therefore, a man shall leave his father and mother and be joined to his wife, and they shall become one flesh. (Genesis 2:24)

Words. What is the value of a word?

Words are important. That is why we are looking at only one word in this chapter: *sex*.

Noah Webster understood the importance of words; his life's goal and commitment was to words. He understood that language is a gift from God, bestowed on Adam at the beginning of creation. He understood that words have the ability to bring life or death, truth or lies, encouragement or despair. He understood the power of words to change and influence society. He wanted to give our new country a firm foundation, so he defined our language for us, and his work has had a lasting impact to this day.

Noah Webster portrait, by Samuel F.B. Morse.
(Image credit: Wikimedia Commons.)

In the introduction to his 1828 *Dictionary*, Webster explained the known history of languages, going back to the historical Tower of Babel.[1] One of the major accomplishments of his dictionary was an accurate tracing of all of our words, whether they originally came from Latin, French, German, Greek, or even Hebrew. For decades, Webster researched the origins of every English word, to make sure that we, as a new country, understood words and their foundations.

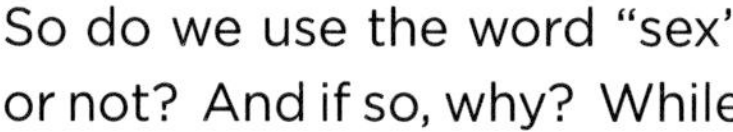

So do we use the word "sex" or not? And if so, why? While writing his dictionary, Webster invented only one new word, *demoralize*—which meant "to corrupt or undermine the morals of, to destroy or lessen the effect of moral principles on, to render corrupt in morals."[2] When Noah Webster's dictionary of 70,000 words was released in 1828, it became the standard by which the citizens of this new nation, the United States of America, would have accurate knowledge and understanding of words.[3] He wanted "a national language as a bond of national union."

Words have changed. What was once "cool" has become "sick"; what was "fantastic" became "bad". In the same way the definition of "sex" is no longer what it once was. The question is, did the word "sex" cause the Sexual Revolution or did the Sexual Revolution redefine the word "sex?" In Webster's 1828 *American Dictionary*, "sex" was defined as:

---

[1] Noah Webster, *An American Dictionary of the English Language* (New York: S. Converse, 1828/modern publication San Francisco: Foundation for American Christian Education, 1967, 1995), Introduction.

[2] Rosalie J. Slater, "Noah Webster's 1828 Dictionary Needed to Restore an American Christian Education in the Home, the Church, and the School," *Noah Webster's First Edition of An American Dictionary of the English Language* (San Francisco: Foundation for American Christian Education, 1967, 1995), 10.

[3] Ibid.

> The distinction between male and female; or that property or character by which an animal is male or female. The male sex is usually characterized by muscular strength, boldness, and firmness. The female is characterized by softness, sensibility, and modesty.[4]

In 1935, the dictionary bearing Webster's name still held to the basic centuries-old definition:

> The physical distinction between male and female.[5]

But we find that after the release of Kinsey's books, *Sexual Behavior in the Human Male*, in 1948, and *Sexual Behavior in the Human Female*, in 1953, the term *sex* was redefined according to Kinsey's fraudulent information. Kinsey has succeeded in redefining *sex*, creating the framework for a revolution.

According to Kinsey's philosophy, the word *sex* has an additional meaning:

> 1) either of the two divisions of organisms distinguished as male or female, 2) the character of being male or female, 3) *anything connected with sexual gratification or reproduction; esp., the attraction of one sex for the other.* (Emphasis added.)[6]

This change has affected the way our society thinks about *sex*, and has aided the transformation to where today we use the word—now referring to every kind of indecency and immorality—in our conversations commonly and unblushingly.

Kinsey was preoccupied with sex and sexuality. For Kinsey and those who embraced his perverted views, man alone was the life-giver. As we have seen, Kinsey believed and taught that "anything goes," and that, because we are "sexual beings", sexual expression must not be limited on any basis, for it is *unhealthy* to exercise moral self-government and be chaste and pure.

---

[4] Noah Webster, *An American Dictionary of the English Language* (New York: S. Converse, 1828; modern publication San Francisco: Foundation for American Christian Education, 1967, 1995).

[5] *New Handy Webster Dictionary* (New York: The World Syndicate Publishing Co., 1935), 424.

[6] *Webster's New World Dictionary* (Nashville, TN: The World Publishing Co., 1974), 679.

Before Kinsey, immoral acts were given different names; they were considered *different acts*...

But Kinsey lumped every kind of sexual immorality together with the marital act, and called it all one word, *sex*, in order to erase the line between righteousness and sin.

| Biblical and Historical Christian Language | Kinsey's Language |
|---|---|
| knew his wife<br>lay with his wife<br>marital act, marital union | sexual intercourse (sex) |
| fornication | premarital sex |
| adultery | extramarital sex |
| incest | sex |
| lay with her by force<br>rape | sex |
| lie with a man as a man lies with a woman<br>sodomy<br>acts of which it is shameful even to speak | homosexual |
| sodomy<br>unnatural acts | oral sex |
| bestiality | sex with animals |
| self-abuse | masturbation |
| molesting a minor with immoral intent | sex education |
| obscenity | pornography<br>harmless entertainment |
| immorality | sexual liberation |
| purity | unhealthy repression of natural desires |
| chaste | repressed |

Kinsey taught us to use a new vocabulary; even in conservative Christianity, biblical language was abandoned under the delusion that "science's" information was more trustworhty than the that of the Bible and historic Christianity.

In days past, it was considered shameful even to speak of the more degrading acts, but just to give you an idea... Consider that prostitution, sodomy, bestiality, pedophilia, and all sorts of other perversions are now called by the same word we use to speak of the holy coming together of husband and wife.

Decades ago, Supreme Court Justice Ruth Bader Ginsburg reflected on how confusing the term has become in today's culture. Speaking to an audience at Columbia University School of Law, she said, "Nine men [on the Supreme Court] hear that word [sex], and their first associations are not what you want it to be... 'Gender' as substitute for 'sex' will ward off distracting associations."[7] And so now, when we speak of male and

[7] "Ginsberg on Sex," *The Washington Times* (November 23, 1993), A5.

female, we no longer even use the word *sex*, but *gender*; and *sex* is reserved solely for the procreative act and every kind of perversion of it.

When, as a parent, the term *sex* is used, what does that term mean to you? If you teach your children to use this term, what will it mean for them? Originally, the definition of *sex* was based on God's Word, as in, "male and female He created them."[8] It didn't refer to sinful acts condemned in Scripture. One hundred years ago, no one associated the term *sex* with marital intimacy, lust, immoral acts, or anything else; it simply spoke of whether something (human, animal, or plant part) was male or female.

Having greater understanding about the origin and importance of words, what terms should parents use with their children today? Where can we go to get the language to communicate sexual truths to our children? God's word has the answer. As we learned stated in Tip 3, nowhere in scripture does God use the term *sex*. In the Bible we can read the terms *know*, *become one flesh*, and *beget*—which all relate to the procreative act between a husband and wife.

God's word promises us *truth*—in this case, a vocabulary we can trust! Speak of this important area of life with your children, and use the appropriate vocabulary with them; use the vocabulary God uses in the Bible.

> As for God, His way is perfect: the word of the Lord is tried: He is a buckler to all those who trust in Him. (Psalm 18:30)

God repeatedly shows us, by His use of the terms, as well as direct commandments, His desire for the Church, the family, and the individual to be chaste and pure. God's interest in purity and chastity lies in His being the true Life Giver and preserver. His ways put society in the best possible position to flourish. And we can see God's desire for us in the very language He chooses to use when He describes intimate issues.

*Chaste* is mentioned in scripture three times, compared to *sex*, *sexuality*, and *sexual intercourse*—which are not mentioned even once.[9] What does the Lord want us to be focusing our attention on? *Pure* and other forms of the word (*purely*, *pureness*, *purer*, *purify*, and *purity*) are mentioned... 130 times!

---

[8] Genesis 1:27

[9] James Strong, *The New Strong's Exhaustive Concordance of the Bible* (Nashville, TN: Thomas Nelson Publishers, 1982), 186, 851.

We have been duped by social engineering. We can learn from God's Word that *sex* has never been His word of choice on the subject of intimate physical relations in marriage, but rather *pure* and *chaste* are His standards. David tells us:

> How can a young man keep his way pure? By living according to your Word. (Psalm 119:9)

It is vital that we teach our children about chastity, purity, modesty, and self-control—all standards that God lays out for us in His Word. In our home, we used the term "marital act" to describe what God intended between a husband and wife. After apologizing to our young children for using the "correct" anatomical terms for the genitals, we switched to using the term "private parts," which stressed modesty and the fact that they were *private* and not to be shown to anyone other than mom or dad or the doctor, if needed.

You may be wondering how parents talked to their children about this subject prior to Kinsey and the birth of sex education. Let's take a peek into my antique books and see what they said about *the flowers, the birds, and the bees.* Communicating in such an indirect way preserved the child's modesty, avoided giving him a sexual identity, and follows the example God sets in His Word. Here's how one author put it:

> She [the mother] may first tell you this beautiful truth, that all life comes from a tiny seed; that before you were born you were growing, just as the seed grows in the ground, or as the bird grows within the egg; that God so planned for your coming that He placed a sheltered nest for you within your mother's body... All human life comes from the father and mother; it is God's way of creating, and the most beautiful way that could be, because a child, having been a part of its parents' bodies, is the more dearly loved.[10]

What a beautiful indirect way of not only relaying God's life process but also stressing God's design for a mother and father to conceive and raise up the next generation. From the same book, here is another example of a parent explaining to a child God's design, in a chapter titled, "How You Came Here":

---

[10] Mary Ries Melendy, M.D., *Vivilore: The Pathway to Mental and Physical Perfection* (W.R. Vansant Pub., 1904), 291–292.

After learning exactly how all the plant, fish, bird, and animal babies come into the world, I suppose you wonder how you got here yourself... You know that you are very different from animals. They have bodies, and life, and instinct, but they have no mind or soul, such as you have. It is because you have a mind and a soul that you are said to be made after God's own image... You heard, did you not, how the male and female bird found each other and how they agreed to make a dear little home for themselves and for their family? Well, when a man is quite grown up, when he is strong and well, and feels that he can earn enough to make a home, he begins to think about marrying, too. As he has a soul, he wants to find a wife with a soul like his, a wife whom he can love and trust. He looks around, and when he meets the right woman—the woman, who has a soul like his—he asks her to be his wife, and come and make a home for him. Then the two are married... At first, your family was a very small one, only father and mother... Mother knew that the souls of people (the masters of their little houses), are sent by God, to live in human bodies. Although she did not know what souls are made of—nobody does know that except God—she knew that the little houses in which they live and grow are made of food and air. Mother knew that in her body, just as in the body of all female animals, there was a little room with a tiny egg, so small that it could not be seen except with a microscope. Just like the bird's egg, it grew and changed as soon as some of father's life fluid got into it.[11]

*The Giant Killer, or, The Battle which All Must Fight*, by A.L.O.E., London: T. Nelson & Sons, 1868.

[11] H. A. Guerber, *Yourself and Your House Wonderful* (Chicago: The John C. Winston Co., 1913) 260–263.

Did you notice that the conversation keeps coming back to God's design and God's life process? God was at the center of families, and God's design for the family was the center point of *the talk*, not the act or the genitals. We see another example from a different book:

> You see darling, father and mother are just two parts of a whole. A home isn't really complete, is it, unless there are both a father and a mother in it? You have to have a father to be strong and brave and true; to take you fishing and to play ball with you, and to tell you about machinery. And then you have to have a mother to be tender and careful and loving; to sing songs to you, and to tell you stories; to kiss the bruised places, and to tuck you into your bed at night.[12]

A simple stroll in the fields and coming upon a flower is a beautiful way to start the conversation about God and His life process. Spend time in God's Word and get to know His patterns in words and what standards He wants us to live by! If words were important enough for one man to dedicate his life to giving our country our own language with its own unique definitions—if words can be used to change history—shouldn't we be using the Word to give us correct terminology for discussing this important subject with our children?

## Remember: Don't Use the S-Word!

> Now Adam knew Eve his wife, and she conceived and bore Cain, and said, "I have acquired a man from the Lord." (Genesis 4:1)

---

[12] Mrs. Woodallen Chapman, *How Shall I Tell My Child* (New York: Fleming H. Revell Co., 1912) 33.

Chapter 6

# TIP 6: TEACH SELF-CONTROL

> People will be *lovers of themselves*, lovers of money, boastful, proud, abusive, disobedient to their parents, ungrateful, unholy, *without love*, unforgiving, slanderous, *without self-control*, brutal, not lovers of good, treacherous, rash, conceited, *lovers of pleasure* rather than lovers of God.
> (2 Timothy 3:2–4)

When seeking God's truth about sexual purity, there's another matter we must consider, an important virtue that has been lost. The act of intimacy with one's spouse is a gift *for* "the other", not a gift for oneself. But today, the act of intimacy for "the other" is being replaced with self-gratification.

In biblical times *knowing* another was the act that sealed the deal; it was the act of giving oneself to another. Throughout scripture we are taught to "prefer one another,"[1] "love one another,"[2] "serve one another."[3] The act of submission is for the purpose of exalting the other; seeking the other's good and not your own.

When it comes to the act of marriage, we desire our children to understand that it is care, concern, and the good of the other that should be

---

[1] Philippians 2:3.

[2] 1 John 3:11.

[3] Galatians 5:13.

driving this train. With this in mind, parents, we need to be prepared to address the act of self-stimulation and the need for self-control.

Let's take the simple task of bathing our children. What is your response when your 3-year-old reaches for his privates during bath time? What about potty training? How do you as a parent respond when your little girl vigorously sleeps with a blanket between her legs?

How do you handle these awkward situations? Whose thoughts are racing through your mind? Is it God and His Word, is it Freud, or is it the illegitimate lies of Kinseyan "science?"

God would want you to remember that we are redeemed sinners in need of guidance and training. Freud would want you to leave it alone and trust that it would go away. Kinsey would have you believe children are sexual beings from birth in need of sexual release, and that as a parent you would be wrong to stop your children from exploring their sexuality.

There are reasons why a young child's hand may go to this area. For example, when they are naked, the hand may find that area and explore simply because it is there; or if pants or diapers are too constricting, the hand may go there. If there is a urinary tract or yeast infection, the hand may also gravitate to this area. These actions do not mean children are in need of sexual release. The key here is not to overreact. With little ones, a simple redirection will do. When one of our children was younger, his hand gravitated to that area while in the bathtub. I gently took his hand and placed it on a toy, and thus I just simply redirected his activity.

Let's take another look at my antique book collection, and see what people were thinking about these matters in the days before Kinsey's fraud became the Gold Standard. But first, a little help with translation: Before Kinsey, self-stimulation was called *self-abuse*.

In 1904, Dr. Mary Ries Melendy wrote:

> The mind, as well as the body, is too often made the victim of self-abuse; and when it starts in the mind the habit is more than likely to extend to the body also... Not only does self-abuse ruin the health and the mind; but it so affects the appearance that, as a rule, all can tell what is the matter... Many have been taught that the sexual organs themselves are impure. This is not true. God made them, and they are the part of the body most sacred

> of all, for to them is given the honor and privilege, under the right conditions, after marriage, of creating life. But certain it is that they must be left alone until that time, except to keep them clean, if they are ever to fulfill this high mission in a way to bring happiness. Let them alone even with your thoughts. It is not wrong to know about them; but I have told you why it is a mistake to keep thinking about them. Let them alone, to grow strong and mature and beautiful in the way that God has planned, and by and by you will be very glad and thankful that you did so.[4]

In 1912, Mrs. Woodallen Chapman wrote:

> From the very first hour of its birth, the baby is being taught either *self-indulgence* or *self-control* through every experience of its daily life... She [a mother] can tell him or her of the sacredness of that part of the body, because it is connected with the bringing in of little children into the world, and the great need of guarding it carefully from all possible harm. Tell the child that those organs are as sensitive as the eye, and would be as greatly harmed by rubbing or other misuse as the eye would be. (Emphasis added.)[5]

Physician John Diggs shares a little medical history on the subject:

> Masturbation is the name given to sexual stimulation of oneself. Medical terminology of previous decades used the term "self-abuse." The term is not far off the mark if one considers that abuse of anything is the use of it in a manner not intended, or not reflecting, its nature. Badminton racquets are not designed to hit baseballs. This is abuse of the racquet. Modern medical authorities and others frequently suggest masturbation as a manner of releasing sexual tension. This "masturbation-is-harmless" attitude was most famously endorsed by the fraudulent reports of one Alfred Kinsey in *Sexual Behavior in the Human Male* (1948), where he argued that repression of sexual desire was dangerous

---

[4] Mary Ries Melendy, M.D., *Vivilore: The Pathway to Mental and Physical Perfection* (W.R. Vansant Pub., 1904), 294-296.

[5] Mrs. Woodallen Chapman, *How Shall I Tell My Child?* (New York: Fleming H. Revell Co., 1912), 41-43

> and unhealthy. Prior to that, the uniform opinion of physicians was reflected in the term "self-abuse."[6]

In *Every Young Man's Battle*, authors Stephen Arterburn and Fred Stoeker address this topic, listing only a handful of the problems associated with habitual masturbation:

- Habitual masturbation consistently creates distance from God;
- Jesus said that lusting after women in your heart is the same as doing it. Since most masturbation involves a lustful fantasy or pornography, we're certain that nearly all instances violate Scripture;
- The pornography and fantasy that surround masturbation change the way we view women;
- Habitual masturbation is hard to stop. If you don't believe it, wait till you get married and try to quit masturbating;
- Masturbation is progressive. You're more likely to masturbate the day after you masturbate than you're likely to do it the day after you didn't. In other words, the pleasurable chemical reactions draw you to repeat the practice more and more. This is bondage, and God hates bondage in His sons.[7]

Dr. John Diggs, speaking from the medical perspective, also wrote of the problems with masturbation; you'll see a lot of agreement between his conclusions and those of Arterburn and Stoeker:

- It is very easy for teens to get into a habit of masturbation that precludes them from doing more productive things that will add to success in their lives.
- Masturbation is a dead end. It wastes time that could be dedicated to more productive pursuits.
- At the same time, the body is being trained to respond to self rather than a spouse.

---

[6] John Diggs, M.D., "Masturbation" (December 13, 2002), available at The Matthew XVIII Group website: matthewxviii.org/articles.

[7] Stephen Arterburn and Fred Stoeker, *Every Young Man's Battle* (Colorado Springs, CO: Waterbrook Press, 2002), 109.

- Sex is a physical and spiritual exchange between two people, a progressive bonding experience, and an expression of intimacy.
- The marriage will not endure if one is more interested in one's self than one's spouse.
- One does not have to be nice to the images in magazines or computer screens. No conversation, no exchange, no investment. No person.
- The risk is run that at some point fantasy will be preferred to reality.[8]

These physicians and counselors did not deny that children show curiosity about their bodies, but this does not support the premise put forth by Kinsey and later by other "experts" on childhood sexuality.

Their view paints quite a contrast. SIECUS published their guidelines in 1991, setting the standards for how and what children are taught in the schools. Not surprisingly, masturbation was *promoted* to children. In these published guidelines, Key Concept 4, Topics 1 and 2 state the following:

> Topic 1—Sexuality throughout Life, Level 1 (Age 5-8): *It feels good to touch parts of the body.*
>
> Topic 2—Masturbation: *Masturbation is often the first way a person experiences sexual pleasure.* (Emphasis added.)[9]

The guidelines further state that many boys and girls begin to masturbate for sexual pleasure during puberty.

As generation after generation has been taught SIECUS's fraud-based curriculum, our people are increasingly ensnared in sexual sin.

In the past few years, legislators have begun to reconsider Kinsey's "findings" and the inclusion of SIECUS's curriculum in our public schools. More and more parents are becoming concerned about the effects of these materials on their children, and the loss of their God-given author-

[8] John Diggs, M.D., "Masturbation" (December 13, 2002), available at The Matthew XVIII Group website: matthewxviii.org/articles.

[9] National Guideline Task Force (SIECUS), *Guidelines for Comprehensive Sexuality Education* (Fulton Press, 1991).

ity to teach their children about self-control. The darkness of Kinsey's abhorrent sex studies on children, at the heart of sex education, is being exposed; and people are shocked at this truth.

But currently SIECUS materials are still the dominant perspective on these matters, both outside and inside the church. And today we find ourselves in a place where a growing number of Bible scholars will tell you that there are no scriptures that directly address the topic of masturbation; *this is not so*. One of the primary evidences of the operation of the Holy Spirit in one's life is the fruit of *self-control!* This is a skill that we must train our children in, just as we train them to be loving, joyful, contented, patient, kind, good, and faithful.

> But the fruit of the Spirit is love, joy, peace, longsuffering, kindness, goodness, faithfulness, gentleness, self-control. (Galatians 5:22–23)

Unfortunately, self-stimulation has become normalized in American culture; comedians joke about it, Facebook has something to say about it, and movies normalize it. Prior to the 1948 sex studies of the Kinsey Institute, Christian society had cherished and upheld sexual integrity, but today many of our youth have been led down the dead-end road of "self-abuse".

Parents must help their children learn self-control, and steer them away from the act of self-stimulation. Your children will bless you for it.

## Remember: Teach Self-Control!

> The Lord God said, "It is not good for the man to be alone. I will make a helper suitable for him." (Genesis 2:18)

Chapter 7

# TIP 7: The True Foundation—Use the Bible to Talk with Your Children

Your word is a lamp to my feet and a light to my path. (Psalm 119:105)

A few years ago, I spoke to a group of church workers about the origins of sex education, its effects on children, and the urgent need for all of us to get back to God's Word. Afterward, the children's minister approached me with many questions, seemingly enthusiastic about the what she'd learned. Her husband, however, who was a pastor at a different church, looked me in the eye and said with disgust, "Is that all? What about all the books on how to talk to your kids about sex? You mean to tell me that I'm to ignore all that, and just use the Bible?" The answer to that question would be a resounding, "Yes!"

The Bible no longer sets the cultural standard for morality in America; yet God tells us that, "All scripture is given by inspiration of God, and is profitable, for reproof, for correction, for instruction in righteousness."[1] In the 1600s, 1700s, and 1800s, the Bible was the primary book used in

[1] 2 Timothy 3:16.

schools in America; today the Bible is banned and disparaged as archaic. Instead, something else has taken the Bible's place, and our children are being exposed to more sexual immorality than ever before in our history.

The Bible has everything we need as parents to teach and train our children about right and moral living. The enemy has plans and a scheme for evil for our children, so it is necessary that we have the help of the One who is infinitely wiser and more powerful than the devil to guard and protect them. And God has the best plans for our children! God's Word is sufficient.

In this chapter we will highlight the differences between God's plan for the moral education of our children and the enemy's plan. We will be looking at the importance of scripture, moral training, and recognizing the lies of our culture in the training of our children.

When our nation turned to embrace man's science over God's Word, we opened the door to men and women with nefarious plans for our children's minds. Those plotters worked diligently to restructure our children's thinking, and they have been extremely successful. How can we fight against them?

> You shall teach them [God's commandments] diligently to your children, and shall talk of them when you sit in your house, when you walk by the way, when you lie down, and when you rise up. (Deuteronomy 6:7)

> Train up a child in the way he should go, and when he is old he will not depart from it. (Proverbs 22:6)

God's commands to parents are not simple things we're going to accomplish with an occasional Sunday activity, or a mad crush for Bible memorization. He requires that we daily ponder His Word, live out His truths, and pour into our children's lives.

This should not be an "us versus them" (the moral versus the immoral) issue, but one of faithfully following a Father who loves us and wants the best for us.

Using God's word is vital in the battle for our children's souls. Priscilla Shirer writes about the importance of the soul, describing it as being made up of four parts: your mind, your will, your emotions, and your conscience. Here is my analogy:

- **Mind**—God's thoughts (His Word) give us peace; Satan's thoughts give us fear, anger, worry, depression, doubt, and lust.
- **Will**—God gives us the ambition to help others; Satan gives us the ambition to focus on self and use others.
- **Emotion**—God can help us control our emotions and gives us compassion and love for others; Satan gives us volatile, out-of-control emotions that dictate actions without thought.
- **Conscience**—God gives us a clear moral compass in His Word; Satan tells us, "Anything goes," and teaches us to ignore our consciences, which will become dull—or worse, hardened—over time.

Shirer stresses the importance of following God's Word for how we are to live, writing,

> When you and I choose not to align our actions with God's truth—when we live in blatant rebellion against His will for us—we leave our heart exposed where Satan can take a clear shot.[2]

I do not want Satan attacking my children, so it is vital that I teach my children God's Word.

In the area of purity and our children's sexuality, here are some topics to emphasize with your children, and a few scriptures you can use to begin teaching them the biblical perspective (which is to say, the truth!) about these things.

## MARRIAGE

The first human institution recorded in the Bible is the holy marriage of one man, Adam, to one woman, Eve, in Genesis chapters 1 and 2.

There are also multiple accounts in scripture where people did not follow God's plan for marriage; in each instance, having more than one wife did not bode well for the husband.

---

[2] Priscilla Shirer, *The Armor of God* (Nashville, TN: LifeWay Press, 2015), 71.

- Genesis 29-30—Jacob and his bickering wives.
- 2 Samuel 12-18—David's family tragedies.
- 1 Kings 11:3-4—Solomon drawn away from the Lord.

There are no accounts of any other type of marriage in the Bible.

**GOD'S LIFE PROCESS**

Here are some scriptures to highlight:

- Genesis 1—God initiated life, and designed it to reproduce after its own kind.
- Genesis 4—Adam *knew* his wife (in the most intimate terms), and generations began.
- Gen. 25:21; 1 Sam. 1:11, 17—God causes parents to have children.
- Ex. 20:1-17; Deut. 6:7—God instructs us how to live our lives.
- Psalm 139:14—God makes each person.
- Luke 12:29—God sustains our lives.
- Hebrews 9:27—God knows the end of our lives on earth.

Adam and Eve in the Garden in Eden.

(Bassano Jacopo, Garden of Eden. Image credit: Wikimedia Commons.)

## PURITY

Remember? *Chaste* is mentioned three times in the scriptures; and *pure, purely, pureness, purer, purify*, or *purity* are mentioned 130 times.[3] I won't list every one of them here, but it is worth the time to study these words, especially *purity*, and learn how it is used in each case in the Bible.

> How can a young man cleanse his way? By taking heed according to Your Word. (Psalm 119:9)

This sort of truth is something our children need to hear often. Is it ever too early to let them know of the Father's love? Is it ever too early to be shepherding their hearts and encouraging them to do well? We don't need to teach our toddlers about all of the evils of pornography. But when we keep our eyes on the larger goal—training them in obedience, and training them to trust and obey God—this will lead to them trusting our words; then, when it is time to begin training about the evils of sexual temptation, their hearts will be receptive to us.

Marriage, God's life process, and purity are topics we should be teaching our children about from the earliest age. It's never too early to teach them about God's good plan, and we will continue to teach our children—diligently—about these things, until it's time to start teaching our grandchildren as well!

Now, for the topics we must teach our older children about, particularly as they enter their youth. There will come a time when, as parents, we need to direct our pre-teens and teenagers—depending on their level of maturity—toward God's ideal for them, and away from Satan's schemes, about pornography, interaction with the opposite gender, lust, and God's design for male and female.

## PORNOGRAPHY

- Proverbs 6–7—The seductive woman and the young man. The man allows the woman, eventually, to lead him to his death. Warn your sons to flee from the seductress (and that would include every woman in pornography!).

---

[3] James Strong, *The New Strong's Exhaustive Concordance of the Bible* (Nashville, TN: Thomas Nelson Publishers, 1982), 186, 851.

- Job 31:1—Righteous Job shielded his eyes so that he doesn't look lustfully on a young woman.
- 1 Corinthians 6:18—We are commanded to flee from all sexual immorality. (Anything outside of the marital act is sexual immorality!) *Fleeing is the key here*, and we are not to stay or tarry for a while.
- Psalm 101:4—We must set nothing wicked before our eyes.
- Philippians 4:13—Through Christ we have the power to overcome any temptation put before us.

**THE STANDARD FOR TREATING THE OPPOSITE GENDER**

- 1 Timothy 5:1—Paul exhorts Timothy to treat all young women as "sisters, with all purity."

In our home, when our sons began to observe the dating world, and the way in which many of their peers acted toward one another, they realized that most young men weren't looking at young women as sisters in Christ or helping to keep them pure. For our daughter, we stressed modesty and not leading men to lustful thoughts.

**THE DIFFERENCE BETWEEN BIBLICAL LOVE AND LUST**

- 1 Corinthians 13—Biblical love.

When speaking to young adults, I write out the characteristics of biblical love listed in 1 Corinthians 13, and then ask the students to list the opposite characteristics (see next page). The comparison of the two, side by side, provides them with a vivid illustration of what lust is. If they are in a relationship, this exercise often helps them realize that the relationship is not based on being *in love* but *in lust*.

**GOD'S DESIGN FOR MALE AND FEMALE**

- Genesis 1:26–27—Creation of man and woman.

- Genesis 2:4–25—More details about the creation of man and woman, including how each is distinct and different from the other; yet both made in the image of God, equally important, and necessary for the creation of new human life.

| Love vs. Lust | |
|---|---|
| **Biblical Love** | **Wordly Lust** |
| Patient | In a hurry |
| Kind | Mean |
| Not envious | Wanting what others have |
| Not boastful | Bragging |
| Not proud | Calling attention to self |
| Polite | Not concerned about partner |
| Not self-seeking | Self-seeking |
| Slow to anger | A time bomb of feelings |
| Keeping no record of wrongs | Holds grudges |
| Telling the truth | Lying |
| Protective | Puts partner at risk |
| Filled with hope | Filled with doubt |
| Lasting | Momentary—never satisfied |

Is it love or is it lust? 1 Corinthians 13 is our measuring rod.

Today, God's Word is being ignored, and our children are suffering great harm for it. Today, even *biology* is being ignored, and our children are being taught dangerous views.

Just a few generations ago we never would have thought there was a need to teach and train our children about issues like pornography, homosexuality, and gender confusion. But the day has come when this has become part of our mandate as parents. We must be hyper-alert about the schemes of Satan. When the Bible was our guide, it also acted as our guardrail and helped shape our society. Especially in this godless society, the Bible will be the guide and guard for our children.

Spend time in God's Word; get to know it well, and teach your children how to use it so they can be equipped to counter the devil's schemes.[4]

To get you started, I'll warn you against several of the most subtle and dangerous lies this culture is trying to sell us, and give you a quick scripture to counter each:

- "If it feels good, do it." Exodus 20:1–17
- "There are no moral absolutes." Psalm 37:27
- "The Bible is old and doesn't apply to us today." 1 Peter 1:25
- "You can be whatever gender you want to be." Deuteronomy 22:5
- "Whatever sex act you do or whatever you decide to dress up in defines who you are." 1 Corinthians 6:9–11
- "Try out every sexual lifestyle available and decide what you like." 1 Corinthians 6:18
- "Love is love." Meaning, "Homosexual lust is the same as the love God designed between a husband and wife." Leviticus 18:22
- "Your rights and feelings trump the Bible and your responsibilities." 1 Corinthians 6:19–20
- "You can get rid of 'it' through abortion." Exodus 21:22–23
- "There is nothing wrong with watching porn." Matthew 5:28
- "If you love someone, it doesn't matter that you're a child and your partner is an adult." Matthew 18:6–7

The list of lies goes on and on, but God's Word never fails to show us the truth. This is why it is vital that we study God's Word and teach it to our children. Are you noticing throughout these passages how critical God's Word is, if we are to survive the enemy's attacks?

Finally, Ephesians 6 tells us that God has given us all the weapons and armor we need for this battle. We need to do battle His way rather than struggle against the enemy with our own strength.

> Finally, my brethren, be strong in the Lord and in the power of His might. Put on the whole armor of God *that you may be able to stand against the wiles of the devil*. For we wrestle not against flesh and blood, but against principalities, against powers, against the rulers of the darkness of this world, against spiritual hosts of wickedness in the heavenly places. (Ephesians 6:10–12)

---

[4] Ephesians 6:11

We are to put on:

The belt of **Truth** (verse 16). Satan comes at us with lies; we hold ourselves together with God's truth. Every human being is His image bearer.

The breastplate of **Righteousness** protects the heart, which is the centerpiece of the soul (verse 14). Our hearts are easily deceived,[5] therefore we must be *diligent* to study God's commandments and keep them.

The shoes of the **Preparation of the Gospel of Peace**; only the gospel of Christ can make us at peace with God (verse 15), and once we have true peace with God, it overflows to every other area of our lives.

The shield of **Faith**, which extinguishes the fiery darts which Satan launches our way (verse 16). This means that we walk in belief of what God has said in His Word, rather than the rhetoric the world wants us to believe.

The helmet of **Salvation**, which is our identity in Christ (verse 17). The function of a helmet is to guard our minds. Having been saved by Jesus Christ who is the very Truth, when the counterfeit presents itself, the contrast is glaring.

The Sword of the Spirit, which is the **Word of God**, that can be used to slay the enemy—be it temptation, deception, or whatever darkness we are struggling against (verse 17). Equip yourself and your children with biblical responses to the lies that they will hear.

## Remember: Use the Bible to Talk with Your Children about God's Life Process!

> For though we walk in the flesh, we do not war after the flesh: For the weapons of our warfare are not carnal, but mighty through God to the pulling down of strongholds: casting down imaginations, and every high thing that exalteth itself against the knowledge of God, and *bringing into captivity every thought to the obedience of Christ.* (2 Corinthians 10:3–5)

[5] Jeremiah 17:9

# TIP 8: When Your Child Asks You Questions about Sex, Ask Him More Questions First

When I was a child, I spoke as a child, I understood as a child, I thought as a child; but when I became a man, I put away childish things. (1 Corinthians 13:11)

When your child comes to you with questions about intimacy, there are two things you should know. First, if he is truly asking, you are late in equipping him with the right kind of information. But, second, it may be that your child isn't truly asking you about intimacy. Before you go any further, you need to play detective. Later in this chapter, there will be samples of conversations other parents have had with their children. But first things first.

It is not uncommon for most parents to avoid "the talk," until one day they find themselves in a predicament where their child comes to them with the big question, "Where did I come from?" Now that you understand where that natural hesitation was coming from, and that teaching your child about God's life process isn't about the graphic details of the marital act, you need not be subject to that dread any longer. From a very early age you can begin sharing truths with your child about how God, in His perfect design, allows things to grow and reproduce. As we have learned, "the birds, the bees, and the flowers" approach is an excellent way to communicate information about how another of the same kind is made.

In my garden, flowers, vegetables, and fruit trees grow. One afternoon my husband and I went over and closely inspected the activity around a large sunflower. We explained to our kids the important work of the bees. Bees fly to flowers to gather nectar, from which they make honey. As they gather the nectar, they brush against the pollen, which comes from the male part of the flower, and some of it gets on them (just the same way pollen will get on the noses or fingers of children!). When the bee flies on to the next flower and brushes against the female part of it, some of the pollen from the first flower gets left behind, and sinks down, down into the flower, where the ovule, or egg, is—and when the pollen joins the ovule, that is the very beginning of a new sunflower plant! The bees, in their happy work of gathering nectar, gather the pollen and take it from flower to flower, aiding in the process of making seeds which will produce more flowers. From that day on, the kids were always very curious to watch the bees wherever they found them congregating; they knew those bees were doing important work.

Teaching your child about the birds and the bees does not totally remove the need to have "the talk." But it does give you, the parent, a launching place for further discussions. Often children will figure it all out by themselves when properly guided along the way by their parent, but there might be some details that need filling in.

When your child asks, "Where did I come from?", first of all, be a good detective and ask more questions. He just may be asking, "What state was I born in, what city did we live in when I was younger, or where do grandma and grandpa live (while telling a schoolmate about his summer vacation)?" Play detective, and ask questions. If they want to know about the baby in your stomach and how it got there, a simple answer of, "All the babies in our home came from a special relationship between mommy and daddy," will usually satisfy in the younger years. If you are honest and they are still curious they will come back with more questions in short order.

Remember, despite what the "experts" say, children are not sexual from birth, and they are usually not hungry for sexual knowledge. In fact, the opposite is true.

If a child is asking many detailed or graphic questions, please know that children are not born with this knowledge. There had to be a source for any graphic sex information they have. Were they exposed to sex education at school or church? Were they exposed to pornography or, worse, sexual abuse by another child or adult? It is imperative that you explore further what your child does know and where he got that information.

Many so-called experts teach that "the talk" should be given before the questions come. They want you to believe, "This is it; my child wants to know all about sex, how conception occurs, and sexual attraction." As a school nurse, having taught many sex education classes, I was on the receiving end of many students' comments. They were very clear about what they thought about the information I'd given them: They thought it was "yucky." In addition, they thought the information disseminated was "gross." Parents, children are not hungry for this knowledge. When these situations arise, start back with Tip 3: Approach the Topic with Modesty, and use that as your baseline.

Sexual knowledge given to children prematurely robs their childhood from them incrementally. The more knowledge children have about the act itself, and the younger they receive this information, the more their childhood is being stolen. When the matter comes up, take a deep breath and remember that these are children, not miniature adults you are talking to. They lack the cognitive maturity to assimilate the whole sexual ball-of-wax!

Here are a couple of conversations that might provide good examples for you. Remember, these are simply suggestions; take them, improvise, use what you can.

I once had a conversation with one of my sons when he was in second grade. He was taking a bath, and I popped my head in to make sure he was okay. Evidently, he thought this was a good opportunity to ask me a question about some graphic information he had heard from a classmate at school. Being a nurse, I could have easily brought out the anatomy books and shown him pictures of the genitals and gone over all the stuff that he had heard. Thankfully, this situation occurred after years of research, and I was well aware that this would be the exact approach that Planned Parenthood and the porn industry would have wanted me to use, and that their way wasn't a biblical approach. So I took a different tack.

The conversation went something like this:

> Me: Do you remember when we talked about the flower and how God designed the life process for all plants, animals, and people? (This took his mind away from any graphic information that was in his head and to a morally neutral object: the flower.)
>
> Son: I remember, Mom.
>
> Me: Did you know that the marital act is such a special gift reserved only for a husband and his wife that God doesn't even mention it in scripture?
>
> Son: No, I didn't know that.
>
> Me: Since it is a gift God intended for marriage, just like a birthday or Christmas gift, God doesn't want that gift opened until the right time, when a man and woman are married. And He also wants you, me, and others to be modest with our words and conversations; meaning that this is not something to be talked about with classmates but is intended for the husband and the wife to talk about when they are married.

My son was relieved, as I gave him some general information about God's life process, put it in the context of why God designed it, and taught a lesson of modesty—by also taking care to be modest in the words I used. I didn't give him information that he was never intended to handle.

Another example is from a friend of mine who told me the following story, from when her son was young. The conversation took place between her son and husband, and provides a beautiful example of how to talk to kids when these sorts of questions arise; I asked her to write it down:

> Our son was taking Catechism, and the topic of adultery and premarital sex came up in the reading.
>
> John prayed before talking to Joshua. When he went in to speak to Joshua, he still had no idea what he was going to say. God is so good, and this is what transpired...

> John told Joshua, "There is a special gift that God gives a husband and a wife to share after they are married. Adultery is when a couple shares this gift and they are not married.
>
> "Let me give you an example about this gift. Let's say that you saved money up for a whole year to buy your brother Tim a bike. You bought the bike and hid it in the basement. The next morning you saw Tim riding the bike. How would that make you feel?" He naturally said that he would feel pretty bad. "Tim opened the gift before he was supposed to," John told Joshua. "That's what people do when they open God's gift before they are supposed to."
>
> Joshua said to his dad, "But I don't even know what that gift is." John's response: "Okay, let's say you bought Tim a bike and you told me everything about the bike: the color, how many speeds, etc. How would you feel if I went and told Tim every detail about the bike? Would that spoil the gift?" Joshua said that it would. John then said, "That is why I do not feel I should explain to you in detail about this special gift that God gives a husband and a wife. I would ruin the preciousness of the gift. You have to trust me on this."
>
> Joshua understood, and he has no desire to hear about sex from others because he doesn't want to spoil the gift. He is still innocent and God is so good. He put those words in John's mouth. God will honor those who seek His will and His way for our lives.

The key to this story is that John prayed for wisdom before talking to his son, and the Holy Spirit helped him. Every child is different, and every situation is different, and the most important thing we can remember to do, in that moment, is to turn to God and ask Him for help, *in that specific situation*. How many times do we pray before we act? In today's dangerous culture it is *vital* that we remember to turn to God for wisdom.

One final example I love comes from the childhood of Corrie ten Boom:

> Once—I must have been ten or eleven—I asked Father about a poem we had read at school the winter before. One line had described "a young man whose face was not shadowed by sexsin."

> I had been far too shy to ask the teacher what it meant, and Mama had blushed scarlet when I consulted her....
>
> So the line had stuck in my head. "Sex," I was pretty sure, meant whether you were a boy or a girl, and "sin" made Tante Jans very angry, but what the two together meant I could not imagine. And so, seated next to Father in the train compartment, I suddenly asked, "Father, what is sexsin?"
>
> He turned to look at me, as he always did when answering a question, but to my surprise he said nothing. At last he stood up, lifted his traveling case from the rack over our heads, and set it on the floor.
>
> "Will you carry it off the train, Corrie?" he said.
>
> I stood up and tugged at it. It was crammed with the watches and spare parts he had purchased that morning.
>
> "It's too heavy," I said.
>
> "Yes," he said. "And it would be a pretty poor father who would ask his little girl to carry such a load. It's the same way, Corrie, with knowledge. Some knowledge is too heavy for children. When you are older and stronger you can bear it. For now you must trust me to carry it for you."
>
> And I was satisfied. More than satisfied—wonderfully at peace. There were answers to this and all my hard questions—for now I was content to leave them in my father's keeping.[1]

You think Corrie's father might have been praying during that pause?

## Remember: When Your Child Asks You Questions about Sex, Ask Him More Questions First!

> Call upon me in the day of trouble; I will deliver you, and you shall glorify Me. (Psalm 50:15)

---

[1] Corrie ten Boom, The Hiding Place (Carmel, NY: Guideposts Associates, Inc., 1971), 30–31.

Chapter 9

# Tip 9: Look at Children through Jesus' Eyes

> Then He took a little child and set him in the midst of them. And when He had taken him in His arms, He said to them, "Whoever receives one of these little children in My name receives Me: and whoever receives Me, receives not Me but Him who sent Me." (Mark 9:36–37)

A classic picture used to hang in our son's room, of Jesus holding a small child and surrounded by other young children. I'm sure you've seen it, or one just like it. We all love to think on that moment; the gospels describe it so vividly, and it is so striking. With a full plate of ministry work to do, Jesus tells all the adults around him to wait, while he gathers a child in His arms and teaches them all how very, very valuable children are in His sight.

Our Lord Jesus viewed children as precious and innocent, going so far as to lay an especially terrible judgment on those who offend the little ones who believe in Him.

> Whoever causes one of these little ones who believe in Me to sin, it would be better for him if a millstone were hung around his neck and he were drowned in the depth of the sea. (Matthew 18:6)

Quite a contrast from the "experts" who see our children as "sexual beings from birth," wouldn't you say?

As a parent, you have fond memories of some of the crazy adorable things your child has said or done. It is a blessing and a comfort to see your child growing and maturing, moving step by step toward adulthood. Keep that love in the forefront of your mind, and realize—Jesus didn't just love some cute little child in that crowd by the Sea of Galilee; Jesus loves *your* child. But more than that, as much as you love your child, Jesus loves him *even more than you do*. He created every wonderful feature of your child, but He also never gets impatient with him, when it comes to the things that aren't so wonderful. His love is perfect, never failing. And it is real, very real.

In God's providence, He chose for you to be the parents of your children (whether natural-born or adopted!). He has called you to a high task, to raise up these children whom He loves so much... but do not fear; He will also fully equip you to fulfill it, if you trust and obey Him.

Our children are depending on us to tell the truth. We need to incite a revolution which would cause attitudes to be changed, and old laws that once protected children to be restored. Can we, as parents, handle the larger battle of our culture well, while preserving the innocence of our children?

Previously we dealt with why you may feel uncomfortable having "the talk" with your children. *Are those feelings of discomfort God-given, or am I just being a wimpy parent?* One time when I was talking with Dr. Judith Reisman about this issue, she said something that made the matter crystal clear for me: *"Audrey, once adults talk to their kids about sex, they sexualize them to themselves, to other adults, and to each other."*

Sexual words and images are powerful. When we supply our children with these words and images, the children will store them in their imaginations; and when those words and images come to our children's minds, they do not have the moral maturity to deal with them properly. We are forcing children to take on the issues of adult sexuality, years before God has designed them to do so.

Gary and Anne Marie Ezzo summed up the problem with giving children sex information too soon:

> Childhood innocence is what keeps a child in childhood. Remove the innate innocence of childhood and you remove the essence of childhood. In our 35-plus years of parent education, we have come to realize that nothing assaults childhood innocence faster, and with more destructive influence, than providing children with inappropriate sex knowledge, before they are developmentally ready to manage such knowledge emotionally, intellectually, and morally.[1]

When Judith spoke to me a lightbulb went off in my head: If we are the body of Christ and the Holy Spirit lives within us, that discomfort we feel is coming from God. God never intended for parents to sexualize their children; they are to protect them!

This duty goes beyond parents, though. The Lord Jesus instituted the Church, in which pastors and elders are given the responsibility by God to equip parents on this issue (as well as many other issues, of course), by warning them against dangers, training them with the wisdom and tools they need, and strengthening and encouraging them to fight to protect their children. We were counting on our church leaders... and it turned out that many of them had, themselves, been led astray.

Do our church leaders still see children through Jesus' eyes, or do they see them through Kinsey's eyes?

Leaders in the church over the past sixty years have not taken a stand for children, but were swept along by the "research", teaching, and training of secular society. To be fair, most Christians in those early days thought of America as a Christian country, and they simply could not fathom the sort of deception and evil that was at work; but nevertheless, they did not measure the new dogmas against the measuring rod of the Word of God, but instead allowed the new ideas into their homes and churches.

The only solution is to get to the root of the problem. Repent, and work toward reversing and repairing the damage done. The church ought to be taking the lead in turning this around.

It is imperative that leaders in the church shift their point of view about children; this is down at the root of the problem. For example, many

---

[1] Gary and Anne Marie Ezzo, *Protecting the Innocence of Childhood* (Mount Pleasant, SC: Growing Families International, 2018), 16.

Christian groups are cropping up to combat sex education and pornography, and I highly commend them for that. However, I recently participated in an online event, designed to help parents dealing with the hypersexualization of their children; and the answers provided were actually directing the parents to use the very techniques that Kinsey promoted! They were instructing parents to talk directly and graphically with their kids about sex. This is, sadly, typical. It must stop!

For the past twenty-one years, many leaders have invited me to offer seminars exposing the havoc Kinsey has wreaked. After every seminar there is always a time for questions and answers. While some parents ask questions openly, others wait until everyone has left. That was the case recently, when a mother approached me and asked a question that literally took my breath away. She explained that she had just adopted two sisters, two and four years old, who had been rescued from sex trafficking. They were put in rooms with men who could do whatever they wanted with them. This mother then asked, "How do I talk to my girls about sex, because they already know what it is?"

The mother explained that she had just adopted two sisters, two and four years old, who had been rescued from sex trafficking.

(Image credit: Emma on Unsplash.)

Taking a deep breath, quietly praying for wisdom, I explained to this mom that her daughters did not know God's beautiful plan but had experienced Satan's plan of lust and devastation. I reminded her that these precious babies are beautiful, holy, and still innocent. I encouraged her to teach her girls about God's plan, and what chastity and purity look like. I encouraged her to start looking at them through Jesus' eyes, not through the eyes of Kinsey or the world. Let us all do the same!

Remember, we have a tool to combat the exploitation of our children, and all sins related to promiscuity, which is powerful above every power raised against it—God's Word. If we can look at our children through Jesus' eyes, we can be motivated to protect them by providing information with a very modest approach, such as telling them about *the flowers, the birds, and the bees*.

For far too long, the "sex experts" have attempted to lead our little ones into sexual sin, and they will meet with a very harsh judgment. In Matthew Henry's commentary on Matthew 18:6, he explains the severity of this crime:

> This word makes a wall of fire about them [children]; he that touches them touches the apple of God's eye.[2]

You can decide for yourself where Alfred Kinsey fits into that picture.

Kinsey's book presents a very different view of children, where the "data" he collected from pedophiles led him to some chilling conclusions:

> ...it must be accepted as a fact that at least some and probably a high proportion of the infant and older pre-adolescent males are capable of specific sexual responses to the point of complete orgasm, whenever a sufficient stimulation is provided.[3]

Along with the help of other academic elites and the media, Kinsey convinced the public that he was the authority on sexuality. Stating that children were sexual from birth, he convinced us that we needed to see children through his (Kinsey's) eyes, and not through the eyes of Jesus. Amazingly, despite the questionable statistics Kinsey gathered, many in our society, even Christians and the churches, embraced his ideas. In 1961, for example, a research team of conservative Christian pastors in the Lutheran church concluded:

> ...Alfred C. Kinsey and his associates were discovering some facts about sexual behavior. Though many doubts have been expressed, both in the press and elsewhere as to the validity of the Kinsey findings, it is probably fair to say that, insofar as statistical studies

[2] Matthew Henry, *Matthew Henry Commentary*, Vol. 5 (U.S.A.: Hendrickson Publishers, 1991), 205.

[3] Alfred Kinsey, Wardell Pomeroy, and Clyde Martin, *Sexual Behavior in the Human Male* (Philadelphia: W.B. Saunders Company, 1948), 160.

> can give us accurate information, the Kinsey books are reliable for the type of study made.[4]

Society and social values are never static, and the many "sexuality experts" that have come after Kinsey have continued to promote his view of human sexuality. You probably remember many of the names from Part I—Masters and Johnson, Lester Kirkendall, Mary Calderone, William Genné, Clark Vincent, Harriet Pilpel, Alan Guttmacher, Ralph Eckert, Evelyn Duvall, Ann Landers, William Cole, Donald Kuhn, James Hymes, James Pike, Karl De Schweinitz, Lester Beck, and Ira Rubin, to name a few; you find these names in textbooks, professional journals, newspaper and magazine articles... everywhere Kinsey's perverted view of human sexuality was being taught. And most are listed in the *Learning About Sex* sex education series for Christian children. Our parents didn't stand a chance at blocking sex education from entering the schools, because once the church leaders were deceived, they went on to lead their flocks over the cliff.

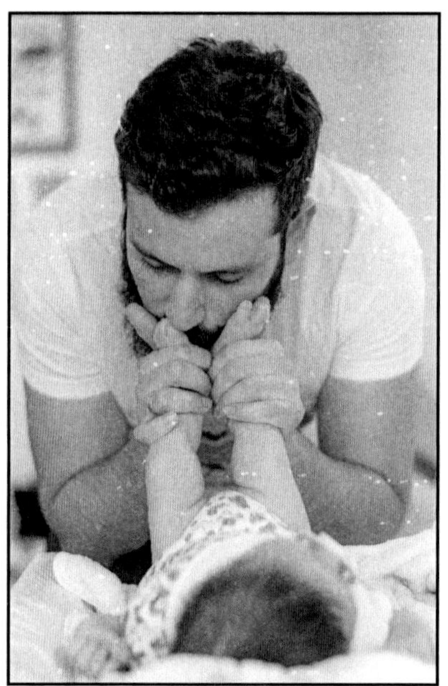

We can bring back the understanding that children are precious and in need of protection, simply by starting with ourselves.
(Image credit: Felipe Salgado.)

Tragically, sex sells. And many people are making a lot of money at the expense of our spouses and innocent children. People are willing to pay for the exploitation of another human being; they have lost sight of each person as an Image Bearer of the Most High God. Exploitation will continue as long as incorrect information is disseminated in society and in the church. What is the part that I can play to stop the spread of these lies?

Only a few generations ago, the people of our society viewed children as vulnerable and in need of protection; we can bring that understanding back in our own homes, in our own churches, and in our own neighborhoods and towns, simply by starting with ourselves.

---

[4] Oscar Feucht, *Sex and the Church* (St. Louis: Concordia Publishing House, 1961), 7.

You can communicate the truths about the act of intimacy to your children that they need to know, in a way that protects their innocence and does not "arouse or awaken love before its time." Start by viewing children—all children—the way Jesus sees them, as precious, infinitely valuable, and innocent. The only way that sex education can be eliminated or changed is when parents no longer look at their children through the human sexuality experts' eyes, but start looking at them through the eyes of Jesus.

## **Remember:** Look at Children through Jesus' Eyes, and not the Human Sexuality Experts' Eyes.

> Then they brought little children to Him, that He might touch them; but the disciples rebuked those who brought them. But when Jesus saw it, He was greatly displeased and said to them, "Let the little children come to Me, and do not forbid them; for of such is the kingdom of God." (Mark 10: 13–14)

Chapter 10

# Tip 10: Make the Purity Paradigm Shift

And I looked, and arose and said to the nobles, to the leaders, and to the rest of the people, "Do not be afraid of them. Remember the Lord, great and awesome, and fight for your brethren, your sons, your daughters, your wives, and your houses." (Nehemiah 4:14)

**THE SEXUAL REVOLUTION CAN EITHER CONTINUE WITH OUR CHILDREN, OR IT CAN END WITH OUR CHILDREN.**

This is my call to action: The Sexual Revolution can either continue with our children, or it can end with our children.

You have been given much information. What are you going to do with it?

Today we stand where we do, not because of one cataclysmic event, like a moral tsunami, but rather, because of the work of many decades—first, to deconstruct the moral underpinnings our forefathers fought to establish, and then, to replace them with a new foundation for our society, one of moral depravity. No single one of us can turn this thing back in a day, but there is something every one of us can do, to defend our little ones against the enemies coming against us, and to rebuild the old walls that once protected our people: Make the Purity Paradigm Shift. When you make the Purity Paradigm Shift in your own heart and life, it will have a ripple effect in your home, community, and perhaps even beyond.

## UNDERSTAND THE ENEMY

It seems like it was a lifetime ago when I became a sex educator. Back then, it was my genuine desire for sex education to be the answer to the problem of sexually active teens. I believed that talking to kids about sex would decrease the pregnancy and venereal disease rates, and create a healthy outcome for all of us.

But, clearly, this was not the case. Every layer I pulled away from the onion of sex education led me one step closer to a truly evil foundation. Time and time again it was made clear to me that many people giving kids sex education *just don't know what they don't know.* For example, a few years ago, a local pastor preached a five-sermon series on sexuality to his congregation; he began by recommending a favorite book he had used as a resource. That book cites in its sources two authors who not only were Kinsey's associates, they openly promoted pedophilia as normal and healthy. This pastor's desire was to help his congregation, but he was feeding them information on sexuality that was written by promoters of pedophilia!

It is time for us to understand the enemy we're dealing with here. Many in the church are using Kinsey's fraudulent science, and they don't even know it.

After the attacks of September 11, 2001, the American people were spurred to turn our attention to our national security, in a way we hadn't had to for decades prior to that day. We were shocked and dismayed that less than a dozen plotters had slaughtered thousands of Americans, with seemingly no security measures having stood in their way.

What many of us did not understand, myself included, is that there was a much greater threat to our national security at play, which had killed far more Americans through the holocaust of abortion, had as its goal the destruction of the free United States of America, and was rendering many Americans impotent to fight against it: *sexual immorality*.

The morality of our nation affects the success of our nation. We need to be clear about who we are following and why! American laws once reflected God's Word; however, those Bible-based laws have been removed, and man-made laws now legalize sex acts that used to be considered unspeakable for their gross immorality. Samuel Adams knew the importance of living chaste and pure lives, and the cost America would pay if this was lost:

> A general dissolution of principles and manners will more surely overthrow the liberties of America than the whole force of the common enemy. While the people are virtuous, they cannot be subdued; but when once they lose their virtue, they will be ready to surrender their liberties to the first external or internal invader.[1]

One of the most famous communist leaders in Russia, Joseph Stalin, understood the pillars of America's strength, and hence what must be undermined:

> America is like a healthy body and its resistance is threefold; its patriotism, its morality, and its spiritual life. If we can undermine these three areas, America will collapse from within.[2]

A person rooted in God's Word can have a successful marriage, healthy children (free of sexual disease and dysfunction), and a closer walk with the Lord.[3] This person has the power of God behind him and cannot be moved.[4]

Scripture tells us that there is nothing new under the sun,[5] and part of our responsibility as parents is to recognize the evil that surrounds our children—whether it is obvious, as it is in our days, or not-so-obvious,

---

[1] William J. Federer, *America's God and Country: Encyclopedia of Quotations* (Fame Publishing, Inc., 1996), 23.

[2] As quoted in the film, *AGENDA: Grinding Down America*, by former Idaho State Representative Curtis Bowers.

[3] Proverbs 2:1–22.

[4] Joshua 23:6–9, Philippians 4:13.

[5] Ecclesiastes 1:9.

like it was one hundred years ago in America. In either case, God is clear regarding what we are to do with those who promote evil:

> And have no fellowship with the unfruitful works of darkness, but rather expose them. (Ephesians 5:11)

Let's review what we've learned. At one time, America was considered a Christian nation. It wasn't because there happened to be more Christians than followers of other religions; we were a Christian nation because our laws and our government were founded on the principles of the Old and New Testaments.[6] Those who opposed Christianity and the Bible did not like this fact. There are numerous biblical accounts demonstrating how easily God's people could be led astray as a result of sexual immorality. And during my research, as you've read, I learned that there was actually a plan to shift America away from our biblical principles, using the vehicle of sexual immorality.

Even after all of these years, the more I study those behind the Sexual Revolution, the more concerned I become. Gabriele Kuby, in her revealing book *The Sexual Revolution: Destruction of Freedom in the Name of Freedom*, summed up why just a few individuals, who are committed to the ideas of humanism, eugenics, and communism, are working so diligently to keep the Sexual Revolution going:

> A person rooted in religion and family is hard to manipulate... Sexualization blinds people and makes them unwilling to resist attacks on the fundamental pillars of society's value system, such as legalization of abortion and homosexual "marriage." Thomas Aquinas said it 750 years ago: "Blindness of the mind is the first-born daughter of lust."[7]

Rene Wormser, counsel to the U.S. Congressional Reece Committee in the 1950s, wrote how the wealthy elite in our nation—the Fords, Carnegies, and Rockefellers—used their non-profit foundations to shape America into their anti-biblical vision:

---

[6] A.M. Dershowitz, *The Genesis of Justice: Ten Stories of Biblical Injustice that Lead to the Ten Commandments* (New York: Warner Books, 2000).

[7] Gabriele Kuby, *The Sexual Revolution: Destruction of Freedom in the Name of Freedom* (Kettering, OH: Angelico Press, 2015), 40.

> An "elite" has thus emerged, in control of gigantic financial resources operating outside of our democratic process, which is willing and able to shape the future of this nation and of mankind in the image of *its own value concept.* (Emphasis added.)[8]

They funded:

- Margaret Sanger
- Alfred Kinsey
- The American Law Institute, which led the states "to gut any laws based on God's Word and offer up new laws that weren't so *repressive*."[9] (Emphasis added.)

These elites understood that a person rooted in religion and family is hard to manipulate. Their objectives were to break the moral bond to God through faith, and the social bond to the family, so people could be seduced by the lure of free sexual gratification. For decades, increasing prosperity made it possible to sell *fun* as the meaning of life, with "sex" front and center. Once the views and behavior of the masses had been altered in this way, the global Cultural Revolution could proceed unhindered through public debate and even open opposition to our Bible-based laws and culture.

Through the work of individuals and organizations committed to ushering in humanism, communism, and eugenics, the Sexual Revolution began to shift a nation away from God's standards. Those who opposed God targeted three areas to be weakened: marriage, manhood, and children:

**Marriage** was targeted because it is the foundation of the family. This was done through the legalization of fornication, adultery, sodomy, and no-fault divorce.[10] Great progress has been made; the ALI's 2001 family court handbook advises jurists:

> Marriage, as currently defined in America, has no status, because it "runs counter to the commitment this society avows toward

---

[8] Rene A. Wormser, *Foundations: Their Power and Influence* (New York: The Devin-Adair Company, 1958), vii–xiii.

[9] Linda Jeffrey, Ed.D, "Restoring Legal Protections for Women and Children: A Historical Analysis of the States' Criminal Codes," *The State Factor* (April 2004), 1–14.

[10] Judith Reisman, Ph.D.; Dennis Jerrard, Ph.D.; Colonel Ronald Ray U.S.M.C.; & Eunice Ray; *RSVP America Training Manual* (Crestwood, KY: First Principles, Inc., 1996), 1–30.

> family diversity."[11] (And remember, this was written before gay marriage became legal; they're declaring that husband-wife marriage has no legal status in family courts.)

**Manhood** needed to be eliminated because Christian men both led their families and protected them. This was done by legalizing pornography in the 1950s, which trained the young men not to prepare themselves to be loving leaders and protectors of future families, but to pursue recreational sex. Men became playboys and women became objects of lust to be used.

> Kinsey's outlet theory ridiculed man-woman love and healthy face to face, eye to eye, lip to lip intimate, and personal heterosexual intercourse. Historian Paul Robinson noted that masturbation and homosexual sex were sexual experiences the Kinsey team touted as better than marital love...
>
> Waving his bunny flag, Alfred Kinsey's most influential general [Hugh Hefner] marched across society. *Playboy* began conquering Judeo-Christian ethics by capturing callow men in college after college, secular and religious.[12]

**Children** were targeted because every good socialist—be he Hitler, Stalin, Mao, or Saul Alinsky—understands that the key to turning a free people into a utopian slave state is indoctrinating children before they are able to reason well enough to understand what's being sold to them. In America, a generation was taught to believe that they were sexual beings through sex education. In 1953, Planned Parenthood officials foretold the fundamental transformation that was their goal with sex education:

> [We must] be ready as educators and parents to help young people obtain sexual satisfaction before marriage... and we must be ready to provide young boys and girls with the best contraception measures available so they will have the necessary means to achieve sexual satisfaction without having to risk possible pregnancy.[13]

---

[11] *Principles of the Law of Family Dissolution: Analysis and Recommendations* (American Law Institute, 2002), 2, 12, 13.

[12] Judith Reisman, PhD., *"Soft Porn" Plays Hardball: Its Tragic Effects on Women, Children, and the Family* (Lafayette, LA: Huntington House Publishers, 1991), 25, 27.

[13] Lena Levine, "Psychosocial Development," *Planned Parenthood News* (Summer 1953), 10.

Today, sex education is one of the foundational pillars needed to continue to propel the Sexual Revolution forward. How important is sex education to the movements that have come out of the Sexual Revolution? Let us look at a telling statement made by the late Alan Guttmacher M.D., past president of Planned Parenthood and a signatory of Humanist Manifesto II. When he was asked how the Supreme Court decision that legalized abortion on January 22, 1973, could be made absolutely secure, Guttmacher responded with only two words:

"Sex Education."[14]

Sex education was once illegal in this country; it was considered "molesting a minor with immoral intent" even to mention the words "sexual intercourse" in a classroom—up to the age of 21 years. Today explicit sex education is taught at public schools across the country.

The souls of our children are being threatened by the culture of the world. What you teach your children (or what you allow others to teach your children) will either propel the Sexual Revolution forward or end it. In a letter to William Smith during the Revolutionary War, British statesman Edmund Burke stated what happens when we ignore the evil before us:

> All that is necessary for the triumph of evil is that good men do nothing.[15]

If we remain silent, if we ignore this issue and allow the sex education movement to continue, we will lose our children to those who believe our children are "sexual beings". We could even lose the right to parent our own children. Books on family law already speak of such things openly:

> Parents can be relied upon to have gender and race biases, so courts must intervene in a family on the child's behalf to determine a child's best interest.[16]

This was a well thought-out plan that was carried forward by just a few individuals, dedicated to creating moral chaos—specifically, to destroy the family and the church. Sex education was an important tool used to

---

[14] *Washington Star News* (May 3, 1973).

[15] William J. Federer, *America's God and Country: Encyclopedia of Quotations* (Fame Publishing, Inc., 1996), 82.

[16] *Principles of the Law of Family Dissolution*, 2.

accomplish this task. The following quote is from a reporter and mom who was concerned with the outcome of sex education in 1972, when at that time sex education had only been in the schools "officially" for eight years:

> If you are just the least bit upset about what sex education has produced so far, think what sex education will be like in the next ten or twenty years with the churches rapidly embracing the new sexual mores...
>
> I suppose if enough religious leaders throw out the Bible, the Ten Commandments, and their own convictions, the prophecy in one of the sex education movies will doubtless materialize and the children will get the message: *"By the year 2000 there will be no more organized religion."* I hope that by now you are asking yourself why such a comment on religion appears in a sex education movie. I'll leave you to puzzle that one out for yourself. The same movie, incidentally, which is part of the *Time of Your Life* series, *also tells children that fathers will no longer have any authority in the home.*[17] (Emphasis added.)

Today, indeed, American churches are on the decline...

> The religious landscape of the United States continues to change at a rapid clip. In Pew Research Center telephone surveys conducted in 2018 and 2019, 65% of American adults describe themselves as Christians when asked about their religion, down 12 percentage points over the past decade.[18]
>
> 51% of adults claim to have a biblical worldview. However, extensive testing through the American Worldview Inventory indicates that just 6% of the adult population actually has one.[19]

---

[17] Gloria Lentz, *Raping Our Children: The Sex Education Scandal* (New Rochelle, NY: Arlington House, 1972), 156.

[18] https://www.pewforum.org/2019/10/17/in-u-s-decline-of-christianity-continues-at-rapid-pace/.

[19] Research conducted by George Barna for the Family Research Council Center for Biblical Worldview (2021), "Perceptions about Biblical Worldview and Its Application: A National Survey from the Center for Biblical Worldview," 4; https://downloads.frc.org/EF/EF21E41.pdf.

...and not only are many fathers not prepared to lead and protect their families, in more than 1 in 4 American homes, there is no father at all.[20]

## UNDERSTAND YOUR RESPONSIBILITY

For a righteous man may fall seven times and rise again,
but the wicked shall fall by calamity. (Proverbs 24:16)

All appears hopeless. But we as the body of Christ can do something, and it begins with our children! There *is* hope; we know that God can turn any situation around no matter how hopeless it may seem.

> For I know the thoughts that I think toward you, says the Lord, thoughts of peace and not of evil, to give you a future and a hope. (Jeremiah 29:11)

If we are going to teach our children purity, we have a fight ahead of us. The schools in America are teaching moral relativism, and even grooming children for abuse.

A school nurse in Chicago sent me a book that has a picture of a boy hugging an adult man on the cover; the title of the book is *Unequal Partners*. This is a program written by Planned Parenthood, meant to be an aid to school officials to help children if they are in a sexual relationship with an adult. Unfortunately, the help offered is not to call the police but something very different:

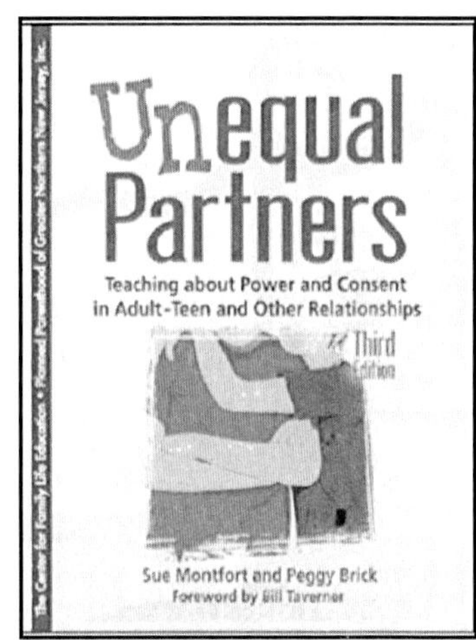


*Unequal Partners*, in use with Chicago children.
(Image credit: Wikimedia Commons.)

> *Unequal Partners* helps teachers, counselors, nurses, and other professionals educate young people (ten to seven-

[20] U.S. Census Bureau. (2020). "Living arrangements of children under 18 years old: 1960 to present" (Washington, D.C.: U.S. Census Bureau), as quoted by fatherhood.org.

> teen years old) to make healthy decisions about relationships, especially those involving the power imbalances that can occur when there are significant age differences.[21]

According to this book, a ten-year-old boy "having sex with" (being raped by) an adult male may not be unhealthy. It is no longer socially *un*acceptable for adults to entice and rape children. Sex education is taking a much darker turn.

God's Word teaches us the opposite of what is being taught by those in the field of human sexuality, the opposite of what is being taught in sex education classes across the country. God not only gives us clear moral guidelines to follow to keep us healthy, He also reminds us of who we are in Him:

> Do you not know that the unrighteous will not inherit the kingdom of God? Do not be deceived. Neither fornicators, nor idolaters, nor adulterers, nor homosexuals ("effeminate" in the KJV), nor sodomites ("abusers of themselves with mankind" in the KJV), nor thieves, nor covetous, nor drunkards, nor revilers, nor extortioners will inherit the kingdom of God. And such were some of you. But you were washed, but you were sanctified in the name of the Lord Jesus and by the Spirit of our God. (1 Corinthians 6:9–10)

God calls us, as His people, to call out those who are in error. Please remember, our responsibility is two-fold; we are called to protect our children and to expose evil.

> And have no fellowship with the unfruitful works of darkness, but rather expose them. (Ephesians 5:11)

As I uncovered more and more material and felt increasingly impressed to speak out about what was being taught within the church, a ministry now called The Matthew XVIII Group was birthed. The scripture which provided the foundation for the ministry is:

> Moreover, if your brother sins against you, go and tell him his fault between you and him alone. If he hears you, you have gained a brother. But if he will not hear, take with you one or two more,

---

[21] Sue Montfort and Peggy Brick, *Unequal Partners: Teaching about Power and Consent in Adult-Teen and Other Relationships*, 3rd Edition (Morristown, NJ: Planned Parenthood of Greater Northern New Jersey, Inc., 2007), xiii.

> that by the mouth of two or three witnesses every word may be established. And if he refuses to hear them, tell it to the church. (Matthew 18:15–17)

When I recently attended a "parent preview night" at a local elementary school in my hometown, I was reminded of how important it is for parents not only to protect their children, but also to expose the evil that is harming them. Although I homeschool, a few of my friends who had chosen to put their kids into a charter school asked me to tag along and hear what would be presented to their fifth grade boys. Although sex education is taught in the schools, usually starting in the 5th grade, it is not mandatory or compulsory in most states, as many have been led to believe.

At the meeting, the teacher bragged about how the school nurse had searched for a program that would not be *too graphic* but would give children the sexual hygiene information that they would need. When she passed around the booklets the children would receive, I watched my friends' reactions. They both immediately said, "This is too much!"

By now you would think the impact of Kinseyan-based sex education would cease to bother me; however, not only was the material inappropriate, but the teacher's calloused approach shocked me and my friends. She first tried to reassure the parents by stating that she had been part of teaching this program to the kids for the last four years with no problems.

But then she made several telling admissions regarding what the program would do to the children (frankly, I was amazed she openly admitted these things at the parent meeting):

> "It will take the kids a few days to get over the shock of it [the information]."
>
> "They [the kids] will be 'shell-shocked' and it will be the quietest day at carpool all year."
>
> "They will feel like they have lost their childhood."

This teacher was so indoctrinated by her sex education training that she saw nothing wrong with shocking away a child's moral innocence or cutting his childhood short. This teacher was right, as we learned in Tip 2; this information *does* cause stress to children and it *does* put them in shock. Remember, sexual words and images make a powerful impression on the brain.

My heart went out to my two friends; they were the only parents in the room to object openly to this content. Another parent tried to convince my friends to put their kids into the program despite their concerns; she reasoned that their children would probably hear the information from the other kids anyway. The same parent stressed that my friends would much rather their children get the information from the "trained sex educator" first. As one of my friends was leaving the room, she overheard the other moms calling both of them "frantic parents."

This is what we are up against. Sex education is so widely accepted that we as parents no longer question it. To object would mean to go against the flow or be in the minority. Currently, there is a push to make it mandatory in more and more schools; it seems to be a tide too strong to swim against.

What would you do if you were in my friends' situation? Both of these moms pulled their sons out of the school not only for the "hygiene class", but also for the day. One of these moms emailed me later to tell me the reasons why she took her son out—and she also made her reasons known to the school officials. Here's what she told them:

1. The material covers sexual reproduction outside the context of morals and modesty.

2. The material is a one-size-fits-all approach presented to *young children* at different levels of maturity.

3. Imparting values and responsibility are my job as a parent, not the State of Texas or the education system. (I don't expect public schools to even hint at God's plan for marriage!)

4. My child is a precious gift, entrusted to me by God, that I am responsible for shepherding. I won't put him in the hands of a stranger to share information on sexual reproduction. The school can teach him his ABCs and 123s, but not this.

Because of broken homes, because of child sex abuse, because we have stopped teaching our children about what it means to be men and women, there is much confusion in our world. The fact that our nation has removed God's Law as the foundation for our moral standard and replaced it with new laws based on Kinsey has not helped. His influence and ideologies are felt everywhere.

Should your children already be involved in fornication, pornography, sodomy, etc., there is still hope! Yes, it will require lots of prayer and lots of love. Many children and adults now see their primary identity as a false "sexual identity" as opposed to being created in the image of God. Entire communities have arisen, held together by a particular sexual identity. From LGBTQ to SMBD, these souls need our compassion and help. As we learn how to navigate this brave new world, let us remember that we are always to demonstrate God's love to the sinner while not condoning the sin. Please love your children unconditionally, but don't ignore God's truth in the process.

> And let us not grow weary while doing good, for in due season we shall reap if we do not lose heart. Therefore, as we have opportunity, let us do good to all, especially to those who are of the household of faith. (Galatians 6:9–10)

## UNDERSTAND THAT THE BATTLE IS GREAT—BUT GOD IS GREATER

...at the name of Jesus every knee should bow, of those in heaven, and of those on earth, and of those under the earth... (Philippians 2:10)

The Sexual Revolution can either continue with our children, or it can end with our children. Yes, the battle is great. But God is greater.

From the beginning, learning about Kinsey-based sex education in my son's elementary school, I have been driven to make the truth known. First in the school my child attended, but it quickly became evident that the entire body of Christ needed to be awakened about this issue.

> And do this, knowing the time, that now *it is high time to awake out of sleep*; for now our salvation is nearer than when we first believed. The night is far spent, the day is at hand. Therefore let us

> cast off the works of darkness, and let us put on the armor of light. Let us walk properly, as in the day, not in revelry and drunkenness, not in lewdness and lust, not in strife and envy. But put on the Lord Jesus Christ, and make no provision for the flesh, to fulfill its lusts. (Romans 13:11-14)

God gave me both confidence and the resources which kept me on a right track and helped to buoy my husband and me during the fire of criticisms we received for speaking out. My husband was forced out of ministerial work in our denomination—his calling and livelihood—due to our position on sexual purity. But God provided for us in miraculous ways, and helped us through every trial.

There have been some incredible moments when God provided and demonstrated His power and direction. Like when the former Inspector General for the Department of Defense and a Louisiana Supreme Court Justice, both godly men, personally thanked me for this ministry and what is being accomplished. Or when Colonel Ron Ray, the former Assistant to the Secretary of Defense under Ronald Reagan and a champion for biblical morality himself, told me that he "had my back."

Last year was one of the most amazing in my twenty-three years of doing ministry. Some highlights included speaking to Texas legislators in Austin, and to top government and church leaders in Uganda.[22] In Uganda, the UN had crafted an agreement with twenty-one African nations, in which these nations would allow Planned Parenthood International and UNICEF to put sex education materials into their schools in exchange for generous "aid" packages—Uganda was letting sex ed into their schools for the first time. After hearing my information, Uganda's leaders immediately began to pull out of this agreement, despite the generous financial incentives they would now be turning down. It just takes my breath away how God can use the most humble of us!

"Who am I? I'm just a mom," was my common refrain to Eunice Ray of RSVP America for many years along the way. She would always encourage me... and then introduce me to some other amazing person. Yes, God can use "just a mom," and He most often takes the simple of this world to confound the wise. He is looking for one who will say, like Isaiah, "Here

---

[22] "Dangers of Sex Education: Audrey Werner's Presentation to the Uganda Parliament Members," at https://youtu.be/q3LLrvcqmhE.

am I."[23] I have learned that when God calls you to a task, He will equip you for that task, often in amazing ways.

Early on, I was advised to get a "prayer shield", a group of people dedicated to praying over me, my family, and my mission. As Satan's plans to propel the Sexual Revolution forward had gone unchallenged for many years, I knew only God could turn this big ship around. In the early days, I prayed, "God, get me to as many people as possible;" but as time went on, I began to pray, "God, just get me to the remnant." And He has.

## UNDERSTAND WHAT NEEDS TO BE DONE

> ...do not be conformed to this world, but be transformed by the renewing of your mind... (Romans 12:2)

What happened to me is that I went through a paradigm shift... actually, a Purity Paradigm Shift. And now, the choice is before you.

Prayerfully consider all of the information you have just read. Spend more time getting to know the God of Scripture, and then be sure to diligently teach the scriptures to your kids. Make the Purity Paradigm Shift in your own heart and mind.

Teaching children and youth about pregnancy and venereal disease has not worked. I believe the answer to the onslaught of the sexual agenda today is to raise up a generation of children who have a firm foundation in Christ Jesus. He is the One who will define their thoughts, actions, and decisions for the future.

Here are steps you can take:

First, Know Your History! Understand why there was a shift from "the birds and the bees" to "the sex talk".

Then...

1. Model purity for your children in all you say and do.

[23] Isaiah 6:8.

2. Maintain your child's moral innocence, not naïveté.
3. Approach the topic with modesty.
4. Remind your children of their identity in Jesus Christ.
5. Use God's words regarding His life process.
6. Teach self-control.
7. Use the Bible as the foundation for all talks with your children.
8. When your child asks a question about sex, ask him more questions first before answering.
9. Look at your children through Jesus' eyes and not the human sexuality experts' eyes.
10. Yes, make the Purity Paradigm Shift in your own mind, in your own heart.

**THE SEXUAL REVOLUTION CAN EITHER CONTINUE WITH OUR CHILDREN, OR IT CAN END WITH OUR CHILDREN.**

## Remember: Make the Purity Paradigm Shift!

Do not be overcome with evil, but overcome evil with good. (Romans 12:21)

# Afterword: Join the Fight!

The state of Texas was concerned. Motivated by political prudence and financial stewardship, a state representative requested my presentation on sex education. He had a political motivation; he and other legislators wanted to block Planned Parenthood from becoming the primary sex educator in all Texas schools.[1]

He had his staff meet with me. I told them the history of sex education, the story I've just told you: who developed sex education, what its original intent was, and how costly it has been for the youth of the last few generations.

The members of his staff were amazed. At the end of my presentation, his chief of staff, realizing that Planned Parenthood had been in the schools since the beginning of SIECUS in 1964, asked, "You don't mean to get rid of all sex education in the schools?" My response was a confident "Yes, I do!"

Parents and others holding this book, I ask that you be diligent—don't just take my word for it, but do the research, and find out for yourself where the Graphic Direct Approach of teaching children about sex came from. Search out older books that were written for parents before this revolution, before Kinsey published his first book in 1948. Discover for yourself who the "sexuality experts" truly were. You will find not all revolutions

---

[1] Texas Freedom Network is an organization, run by former Planned Parenthood leader Cecile Richards, that tracks all the school districts in Texas regarding their sex education classes, https://www.sourcewatch.org/index.php?title=Cecile_Richards, https://web.archive.org/web/20170920084505/http:/a.tfn.org/site/PageServer?pagename=involved_activist_tools_SHAC&AddInterest=1282.

are fought on battlefields, and not all revolutions are fought for political power. This revolution is motivated by lies and deception, and it has lured us away from the biblical principles God laid out for us in His Word.

My friend Heather McEwan has spent years informing parents in her native country of Australia about the origins of sex education. In one of her presentations, she beautifully encapsulated the vision we should all have for our youth:

> I have a vision of a group of youth... Girls who so know their value, they keep their virtue for whom it is intended... Boys who through courage and Godly revelation of manhood can withstand the cultural tide and retain their virtue also... Young people who are immersed in the job of growing up—to learn, to find their place in the world, to seek out God's plan for their lives rather than be preoccupied by a progression of temporary romantic entanglements.[2]

Let's start a trend with our own children. Let's deal with our past, raise a generation of children who strive for purity, and hence, change the course of our nation and the world!

Today parents all over the world are speaking out against sex education, mobilizing action groups, and forming not-for-profit organizations to equip others. Start with your own home, then take a look in your own backyard. Now that you have undergone the purity paradigm shift, you can share what you've learned with others in your circle of influence who are desperately in need of this knowledge.

> Therefore my people have gone into captivity, because they have no knowledge; their honorable men are famished, and their multitude dried up with thirst. (Isaiah 5:13)

People around us are in captivity, famished, dried up with thirst; let's give them a drink.

---

[2] Taken from a PowerPoint presentation titled "The Fish Presentation," by Heather McEwan, Australia.

# RESOURCES

There are a few organizations leading the way in this fight; check them out for more information, news about the battle, and opportunities to get involved further.

**Protect Child Health Coalition.** This organization not only educates parents on issues related to the indoctrination of children on sexual matters, but they provide tools to fight sex education in your area.

protectchildhealth.org

**Family Watch International.** This organization works at the United Nations to protect and promote the family as the fundamental unit of society, through education, pro-family advocacy, and family-based humanitarian aid. They promote traditional marriage, safeguard parental rights, defend human life, uphold religious liberty, and protect the health and innocence of children.

familywatch.org

**The Matthew XVIII Group.** My own ministry—a purity paradigm for our homes, churches, and nations—provides education and training for parents, pastors, youth, and other organizations all over the world.

matthewxviii.org

**Mass Resistance.** This pro-family activist organization provides information and guidance to people who are called to confront the assaults on traditional family, school children, and the moral foundation of society. This organization is based in Massachusetts, but has supporters and activists in all 50 states, Puerto Rico, and several foreign countries.

massresistance.org

# Epilogue: Is There Hope?

We were all born in the middle of the Sexual Revolution... I know this material can be challenging for us.

This information can be shocking and could anger you, as it did me. After I attended my first RSVP America training and learned who was behind the Sexual Revolution, the leaders' intent, and the evil within their foundation, I lost several nights' sleep.

Nineteen years ago, my son was entering Kindergarten when I was beginning this battle against sex education in the Lutheran church. But fifteen years later, when I was finishing the first edition of this book, I was helping to plan his wedding, with his bride-to-be. Let me share his story.

His story fills me with hope for the future. He had committed himself to maintaining his purity, even as a single man in this culture filled with temptations. He joined the Coast Guard, where he faced seemingly constant teasing from his fellow shipmen for being the lone virgin on his vessel; still, some admired his self-control.

In 2017, he took an assignment to a remote island off the coast of Alaska, so his search for the perfect bride would have to wait even longer, til he completed this tour and could return to "civilization". In addition to teaching our children about chastity, purity, modesty, and self-control, my husband and I had always taught our children that God has chosen the person whom they will marry, and that in God's timing He would bring them together; and that until that time, they were to focus on what God wanted them to do on this earth and live their single lives in purity for

Him. We continued to pray for our son to stand strong in the faith, in spite of the pressures from his crewmates.

But then, the most surprising thing happened. Thousands of miles from home, in a remote part of the world... he found his lifemate.

I had never dreamed he might meet his future soulmate during that tour of duty, but I was proven wrong. God can match the two people He has planned to spend their lives together, even in the most secluded places on His planet!

It was pure joy to watch my son find a lovely young Christian woman who had also committed *herself* to purity, court her, then propose, and finally marry her three months later. Two young people, committed to the Lord and to purity, began a new relationship with no sexual baggage, and none of the guilt that goes along with it. Praise the Lord!

I have been honored and blessed to speak to parent groups all over the country. Often, after hearing of the plan behind the attack on our children and our nation, parents will ask me, "What can I do to fight this?" My answer every time: "Raise up your children in the fear and admonishment of the Lord. Teach your children about purity and how they can honor God, their families, and themselves with their words and actions." Parents, gird yourselves for the revolution that you can be a part of, simply by obeying God in how you raise your children.

May this beautiful prayer from *The Soldier's Prayer Book of 1861* help you prepare for battle, as it has me:

> O MOST powerful and glorious Lord God, the Lord of Hosts, that rulest and commandest all things; thou sittest in the throne judging right; And therefore we make our address to thy Divine Majesty, in this our necessity, that thou wouldest take the cause into thine own hand, and judge between us and our enemies. Stir up thy strength, O Lord, and come and help us; for thou givest not always the battle to the strong, but canst save by many or by few. O let not our sins now cry against us for vengeance; but hear us thy poor servants begging mercy, and imploring thy help, and that thou wouldest be a defense unto us against the face of

> the enemy. Make it appear that thou art our Savior and mighty Deliverer, through Jesus Christ our Lord. Amen.[1]

Amen.

[1] Colonel Ronald Ray, J.D., *Endowed by Their Creator: A Collection of Historic American Military Prayers: 1774–Present* (Crestwood, KY: First Principles Press, 2012), 44.

# Acknowledgments

for the First Edition

First, I want to thank our Lord and Savior Jesus Christ—He uses the simple to confound the wise, the weak to defeat the strong. I pray God uses this book to take on man's view of human sexuality and destroy the lies and deceit at the foundation of the sexual revolution—specifically sex education.

I want to thank my husband Joe who has been my protector and encourager even when this ministry has been costly for the family, and my children who have been my inspiration and hope for the future.

To the many friends and colleagues who helped me throughout the process of gathering information for this book:

- Eunice Ray, founder of RSVP America, who spent countless days equipping me (and others) to take on the Kinsey legacy in the world;
- Colonel Ronald D. Ray, USMC (ret.)—Deputy Assistant Secretary of Defense during the Reagan Administration, Founder of First Principles Press, and author of such historical materials as *Endowed by Their Creator: A Collection of Historic American Military Prayers: 1774–Present*. He has been an invaluable encourager to me and has been a courageous patriot for America;

- Dr. Judith Reisman and Dr. Linda Jeffrey who took time training and teaching me about the sexual revolution and how Kinsey's teaching has negatively affected our laws and culture;

- Gary and Anne-Marie Ezzo of Growing Families International whose courses have helped my husband and me raise children who have a heart for the Lord. They have also been wonderful supporters of my message and ministry;

- To the women who have gone before me to expose the origins and dangers of sex education: Claire Chambers, author of *The SIECUS Circle*; Randy Engel, author of *Sex Education—The Final Plague*; Karen Booth, author of *Forgetting How to Blush*; Gloria Lentz, author of *Raping of Our Children: The Sex Education Scandal*; Linda Bartlett, author of *The Failure of Sex Education in the Church: Mistaken Identity, Compromised Purity*; Dr. Miriam Grossman, author of *You're Teaching My Child What?*; and Mrs. Woodallen Chapman, author of *How Shall I Tell My Child?*

I also want to thank my friends and prayer partners who have prayed for, encouraged, and supported me in this surprising journey. Your friendship has meant more than you can possibly imagine!

Lastly, I want to thank Karen Lindwall-Bourg of Rhema Biblical Counseling Center and Jimmy and Diana Richards for their support and encouragement in writing this book. This book would not have been possible without you!

# Acknowledgments

for the Second Edition

First, I want to thank our Lord and Savior Jesus Christ. I began this journey by saying, "I'm just a mom," but God continues to use the simple to confound the wise, the weak to defeat the strong, and I stand in awe and amazement at the journey He has had me on and how He taken me to places I never imagined I would go. He doesn't call the equipped, but I can attest to the fact that He will equip the called!

I want to thank my husband of thirty-five years, Joe, who has been my protector and encourager even when this ministry has been costly for our family; and my children and grandchildren, who have been my inspiration and hope for the future.

To my many friends and colleagues who have helped me throughout the process of gathering information for this book:

- Eunice Ray, founder of RSVP America, who spent countless days equipping me (and others) to take on the Kinsey legacy;
- Dr. Linda Jeffrey, researcher for RSVP America, who took time to train me on the changes to American law based on the Kinsey "science."
- Gary and Anne Marie Ezzo of Growing Families International, who have been mentors in our parenting and an invaluable resource in Biblical parenting for the world. To Anne Marie, who spends time mentoring me in my ministry and encouraging me.

- The friends who have watched, listened to, and encouraged me on my journey throughout the years—couldn't have done this without you: MI—Pat, Linda, Jean, Mary & Dale; IN—Sandy, Rhonda, Cindy, Dick and Betty; TX—Letha, Rebekah, Diana, Jerri, Debbie, Monica, Tom & Bea Ann.

- Patricia Lentz, Roel & Robyn van Eck, who have spent countless hours helping me to add more content to and revise the first edition of this book.

- To the many women who have gone before me to expose the origins and dangers of sex education: Claire Chambers (author of *The SIECUS Circle*), Randy Engel (author of *Sex Education—The Final Plague*), Karen Booth (author of *Forgetting How to Blush*), Gloria Lentz (author of *Raping of Our Children: The Sex Education Scandal*), Linda Bartlett (author of The *Failure of Sex Education in the Church: Mistaken Identity, Compromised Purity*) Dr. Miriam Grossman (author of *You're Teaching My Child What?*), and Mrs. Woodallen Chapman (author of *How Shall I Tell My Child?*).

Finally, I want to thank the two most powerful warriors in America who fought the good fight and received their reward in heaven this past year:

- Colonel Ronald D. Ray, USMC (ret.)—Deputy Assistant Secretary to the Department of Defense during the Reagan Administration, Founder of First Principles Press, and author of such historical materials as *Endowed by Their Creator: A Collection of Historic American Military Prayers: 1774-Present*. He was a warrior who showed me the plan to destroy a Christian nation and encouraged me at some of my lowest points. He was a patriot that fought for this nation in Viet Nam, DC, and across this great land.

- Dr. Judith Reisman, of the Institute for Media Education—Leading expert on Alfred Kinsey, who passed "the Sword" onto others to carry on her work, and I am honored to be one of them! She was known as a Titan who she never gave up on fighting for children. She was hated by pornographers, abortionists, and pedophiles, and loved by those of us who needed to know we were not crazy for standing against sex education. Her mission is done and she has left quite a legacy for many of us to carry on the work.

# Figures & Illustrations

# Index

## C



## D



## E

## F



## G



## H

## I



## J



## K



## L

## M



## N



## O

## P



## R



## S

## T



## U



## V



## W



## Y



## Z

# About Audrey

Audrey Werner is the founder and president of The Matthew XVIII Group, whose goal is to restore purity to our homes, churches, and nations through education via public speaking engagements, online articles, and other printed materials. This ministry uses the Matthew 18:15–17 process to approach Christian leaders who are using Kinsey's fraudulent and criminal "science," with the hope that once error is identified, Kinsey's works can be purged from Christian resources. As a former public and private school sex education teacher and STD/HIV nurse, Audrey saw first-hand the dangerous outcomes of teaching sex ed to children. Because of this background and her extensive research, she is now known as the "Sex Education Expert" about Christian sex education programs for the Advisory Board of the American Academy of Biblical Counselors and for the Expose Comprehensive Sex Education (CSE) Coalition.

She was certified by the Michigan Department of Public Health in HIV counseling and testing, and by the CDC for STD counseling, testing, and treatment. Her clinical experience also included pregnancy testing and counseling of teens, as well as distribution of birth control to minors without parental consent. Audrey is a national speaker for RSVP America, which is a campaign that was designed to respond to America's spiraling societal decline in the second half of the 20th century. The mission of RSVP America is to restore social virtue and purity to America by educating and equipping grassroots activists to affect law, legislation, and public policy at all levels of government. (The Matthew XVIII Group ministry is an offshoot of RSVP and serves to work directly with the Christian Church.)

Audrey has worked with leaders from Concerned Women for America of Missouri, Texas Eagle Forum, Right to Life SW Indiana, Nebraskans for Founders' Values, Texas Family Association, American Family Association, Family Life Network—Uganda, and Purple for Parents—Indiana on matters related to the root of sex education. Audrey has testified on the history of sex education before Texas Legislators, Texas State Board of Education, Indiana Senate Committee on Education, and Uganda Parliament members. Currently, she serves as Dean of Life Issues and Professor at Master's International University of Divinity, where she teaches courses on sex education and the sexual revolution. Her students include pastors and other faith leaders from all over the world. Audrey will be in the cast of the upcoming movie *The Mind Polluters*, a film about the sexualization of our children which is being directed by Mark and Amber Archer of Fearless Features. This film will be released Fall 2021.

Audrey has been married for thirty-five years to her husband Joe, who served as the Director of Christian Education in the Lutheran Church Missouri Synod for twenty-five years. Together they have four children and one daughter-in-law, and two grandchildren.